TEXTBOOK OF DENDROLOGY

TEXTBOOK
OF
DENDROLOGY

Dr. Shubhrata R. Mishra
Dept. of Botany
Vikram University
Ujjain (M.P.)
(India)

D P H

DISCOVERY PUBLISHING HOUSE PVT. LTD.
NEW DELHI-110 002

Published by:
Namit Wasan

DISCOVERY PUBLISHING HOUSE PVT. LTD.
4383/4B, Ansari Road, Darya Ganj
New Delhi-110 002 (India)
Phone : +91-11-23279245; 23253475; 43596065
E-mail : discoverybooksindia@gmail.com
discoverypublishinghouse@gmail.com
namitwasan9@gmail.com
web : www.discoverypublishinggroup.com

First Edition: **2010**

Reprinted: **2017**

ISBN: 978-81-8356-550-9

Textbook of Dendrology

Printed at:
Infinity Imaging Systems
Delhi

Preface

Dendrology is basically a science all about trees and other plants that have woody structures. It seems appropriate to have such a complicated science for a plant system that took a long time and a lot of effort to evolve into the structures that they are today. Trees have a long history, about three hundred and seventy million years in the making, so there is a lot to learn, and piece by piece the science of dendrology has put together an evolutionary pattern, one that we will likely see continue with new species come and older species die off. The tree is quite fascinating, so too is the science of dendrology if you look beyond it's complicated name and the simple appearance of a tree.

Trees are easy to identify in general terms because they are set apart in the way that they have one woody trunk leading to a whole system of woody branches and support systems, but if it hadn't been for people who study dendrology we might not know how to distinguish one woody plant from another. With over 100,000 different species of trees, dendrology is a huge area of study and it's a massive undertaking to try to learn more about each species than what meets the eye, and also attempt to find and identify new species of trees all the time.

Dendrology deserves to have a lot of interest because trees are so vital to our existence. The average person may not realize how truly spectacular the trees in their backyards are, they add a lot to our environment, and if trees were gone tomorrow our world would change in an instant. Through dendrology we can learn more about the trees that impact our lives in such big ways, and even learn new ways of protecting our existing trees and making the lands more hospitable for new trees and new tree species.

Without dendrology we might take trees for granted, and not recognize what truly remarkable structures they are. Through these sciences we'll continue to learn more so we can care for our trees and other woody plants to the best of our ability.

—**Author**

Contents

CHAPTER 1

Introduction

Dendrology is the study of woody plants; typically trees but there are other thing such as shrubs and vines that also bare similarities to trees so they are studied as well. Dendrology is a science that studies, identifies, and even names plants that have woody structural systems. These woody systems hold a lot of information about the tree, about the evolution of the tree, and how we can best care for and protect each species of tree. Dendrology may not seem like the most interesting science at first glance, but it is grossly complicated and interesting.

Trees are easy to identify in general terms because they are set apart in the way that they have one woody trunk leading to a whole system of woody branches and support systems, but if it hadn't been for people who study dendrology we might not know how to distinguish one woody plant from another. With over 100,000 different species of trees, dendrology is a huge area of study and it's a massive undertaking to try to learn more about each species than what meets the eye, and also attempt to find and identify new species of trees all the time.

Dendrology deserves to have a lot of interest because trees are so vital to our existence. The average person may not realize how truly spectacular the trees in their backyards are, they add a lot to our environment, and if trees were gone tomorrow our world would change in an instant. Through dendrology we can learn more about the trees that impact our lives in such big ways, and even learn new ways of protecting our existing trees and making the lands more hospitable for new trees and new tree species.

Dendrology is a science that studies every part of every single tree. This information allows scientists to understand the root structure, why the leaves are the shape that they are, why the tree may bloom when it does, and even where the tree originated from and what other species it may be linked to.

To a dendrologist, a tree is not simply a simple part of nature; a tree is a very complex structure that deserves extensive examination to understand it, and all trees a little bit better. This is not a job that would be fun for everyone, but the people in the dendrology field are typically very dedicated to their work, and often travel all over the world to see new species of trees and help figure out what makes them work. It's painstaking work, but it's worth the effort.

Dendrology is basically a science all about trees and other plants that have woody structures. It seems appropriate to have such a complicated science for a plant system that took a long time and a lot of effort to evolve into the structures that they are today. Trees have a long history, about three hundred and seventy million years in the making, so there is a lot to learn, and piece by piece the science of dendrology has put together an evolutionary pattern, one that we will likely see continue with new species come and older species die off. The tree is quite fascinating, so too is the science of dendrology if you look beyond it's complicated name and the simple appearance of a tree.

Without dendrology we might take trees for granted, and not recognize what truly remarkable structures they are. Through these sciences we'll continue to learn more so we can care for our trees and other woody plants to the best of our ability.

A tree looks simple when you take just a quick look. You might not see anything remarkable when you look at the trees in your yard, for we have begun to take them for granted. A tree is actually quite complicated and could be defined as a large woody plant with a substantial root system. These perennial woody plants are usually at least twenty feet high at maturity, although there is no set height for what a tree is and what is not. A tree also has a complicated set of secondary branches that are supported by one main stem or trunk. When you compare a tree to other plant systems, trees have a very long life span. Many trees get very tall and will live for very long periods of time.

Simply put, a tree is an organized system of branches upon a single trunk. While you might not think this is significant, if you look around at other plant structures you'll realize that it is unique unto itself, which makes it significant. There are no other plant structures that have this organized system of roots, a trunk, and branches that continue to grow and live year after year all the while getting taller and fuller. What's even more remarkable is that these complicated woody plant systems grow to be beautiful and even produce food and shade to other plants and animals in the area. This is no small task, it doesn't matter how you look at it when you think about that!

A tree is a major part of our ecosystem, and has been for the last three hundred and seventy million years. A tree provides the environment with the ability to cleanse the air, oxygen, and also disperses nutrients into the air for all plants and animals to live healthy lives. Trees are responsible for all other plant life and new species that come to be, as it was the root structures of trees that first made the ground soft and pliable enough for other plants to take root. If it hadn't been for trees, there may not be much plant life at all, if any, except in the ocean.

Trees are something that we often take for granted because we really don't have to think much about them because rain or shine, there they are. It isn't until a tree dies or has to be cut down that we might take notice of it and realize how much we appreciated its presence. Face it, when you are talking about a tree it's easy to overlook its beauty and all the benefits it brings to our environment and us.

The most obvious benefit of trees is the clean air and oxygen they put into the air. Without trees, our air quality wouldn't be near what it is. At a time where our pollution is way out of hand anyway, it's hard to imagine what our lives would be like without all the plants and trees helping to purify the air for us. When you think about the fact that trees just might help us breathe better, it's a big reason to really take the time to care for our trees, giving them the loving care that they need to stay healthy and strong, and keep safeguarding our health in a number of ways.

Another benefit of having trees is that they bring us many wonderful fruits. Without trees, we wouldn't be able to eat and enjoy many of the fruits that we have come to be very familiar with over the years. Year after year there are trees that provide us with apples, oranges, grapefruit, peaches, apricots, pears, cherries, and even more. There are so many fruits that come off of trees that we would be lost without them! Part of our dietary plan would be completely wiped out if we suddenly didn't have any more trees.

Trees also provide many animals with home and respite from the elements. Without trees, many of nature's most beautiful creatures wouldn't have a safe place to go to have their young, to rest, and reproduce. Without these animals we wouldn't have the balance in nature that we currently do, and we all know how important the natural balance is.

There are over one hundred thousand species of trees that are known and recognized by dendrology experts. Every tree species is unique and it requires certain things to survive. All things in the environment around a tree have to be exactly right for the tree to grow, and continue to grow in a healthy way for the course of its life. If just one thing is off, the tree will not grow at all, or it will become infected with pests or infections and eventually die. The need for balance is unique which means every tree is unique, so different plants grow in different areas to fulfill their own unique needs.

One of the primary reasons that different trees grow in different places is the need for water. Some trees require a large or consistent amount of water, so they'll grow in areas of the country that get adequate amounts of rain water to keep the plant healthy and alive. These plants will not be found in areas that don't get enough water, because they simply could not survive to adulthood where they'd be found. Likewise, there are plants that cannot handle a lot of water so they'll be found in areas that get very little water, or they can easily get by with inconsistent amounts of rainwater. The water needs of each plant are very specific, and usually, you cannot get a tree to grow somewhere that does not get enough rain to sustain the plant. If you do get the tree to grow, you'll likely have to nurse it along, and even then, there isn't a guarantee that it will continue to grow. Water is one of the most important elements for a tree to grow, and that is why there can be such a difference in tree species from location to location.

Another of the primary needs of a tree is soil content. Some trees need very nutrient rich soil and they will usually not grow in anything but this very nutrient rich soil. Some areas of the world have a very rich soil content that lends itself to the growth of the trees that require this type of soil. Yet, there are trees that do not need a very rich soil content at all.

CHAPTER 2

Trees

INTRODUCTION

Trees are woody plants with a trunk. Shrubs are also woody but have no trunk with the branches more or less at ground level. It is easy to distinguish the two as trees have a crown at the top and shrubs have a crown closer to the bottom. There are many types of trees: large and small, stout and slender, erect and weeping and evergreen and deciduous. Over the centuries of cultivation and with propagation we now have a great assortment of trees offering considerable choice for landscapers, park planners and the gardening home owner. Trees are usually quite distinguishable from one another even during the winter when they can be recognised by their bark, twigs and branches. No one tree is the same as another even if it is the same species. Their rate of growth, shape and ultimate size will all be determined by their position and climatic environment.

The changing seasons are reflected by the leafy and leafless phases in the life of the deciduous tree. In the spring, as the weather gets warmer, new sets of leaves grow covering the tree with bright green foliage. During the summer the leaves absorb and use the energy of sunlight to produce organic food materials; this process is known as photosynthesis. Each leaf contains the substance chlorophyll, with the light energy, makes chemical substances which are retained and can be released as energy for growth or to build up the tree. Carbon dioxide which is present in the atmosphere is combined with water absorbed by the roots to form energy rich sugars. Together with mineral salts, which the roots absorb, an intricate chemical process takes place and forms the trees substance, i.e. wood, roots, seeds, and leaves.

In the Autumn the leaves provide mobile food material. They change colour from green through to orange and then, after their work is done, they fall from the branches, leaving behind them small leaf scars. At this stage the tree has already made preparations for the new leaf growth. On the ground, the fallen leaves decay and produce a rich mineral nutrient mould which feeds the trees roots. Evergreen trees have a longer life cycle. Each leaf lasts for several years. Each year new ones are added and a few of the older ones fall but the tree never becomes leafless.

This growing process produces a cycle of moisture demand from the ground, greater in the summer and less in the winter, and on clay this alters the volume of the ground and can cause subsidence. Beautiful though they may be it is necessary to make sure that trees on your land (and your neighbour's) contribute to the environment without damaging properties. Leafy suburbs, residential tree-lined avenues and wooded gardens are a inherent and integral part of our "green and pleasant" land. But beware the dangers! Large trees spread out and their roots can quickly become entangled with house foundations. Worse still - a tree's search for water can suck moisture from the ground leaving clay soils shrinking. This causes a lack of support to a property's foundations and can lead to subsidence.

A mature deciduous tree can draw up to 50,000 litres of water a year from the surrounding soil. Biggest culprits are Willows. They look great but the best place for them is at the bottom of the garden - at least 11m from your house. Other large water users are Poplars, Elms, Oaks, Horse Chestnuts, Planes and Ash. Among those that can be planted nearer to your home - but not too near! - are Magnolia, Yew, Holly, Laurel, Spruce and Pine.

Keeping the problem of a trees location in the relationship to a building in perspective is very important. Leafy suburbs, residential tree lined avenues and wooded gardens are an inherent and integral part of our environment. In both town and country they enhance the amenity and give colour and form with the passing of the seasons. However, the eventual size, species and location should be taken into consideration.

Inappropriate species planted near to building should be avoided. The right tree for the right place should be the balance which we look for. Even if a tree is close to a building it may not necessarily cause a problem. There are, for instance, many thousands of oak trees within 8 metres that have existed for many decades and do not cause such damage. We should never jump to any conclusion that trees are always the culprit for a building's ills. The age and method of construction and the way it has been maintained are of equal importance.

The wisdom of retaining a particular species, together with the overall tree health should be considered where trees are particularly abundant or close to the property of a certain age. Many arboriculturalists will have received training in the methods to advise you on these matters. There are no hard and fast rules of assessing the risk of damage that tree growth close to a building will do. Because of the immense number variable factors that take place in the process, making predictions is fraught with difficulty. This is where the application of a little common sense is called for! If there are large trees near your house, and by large we mean over 8 metres (26 ft.) and by near we mean 10 metres (33 ft.) serious consideration should be given to regular pruning particularly if you live in an area where there are clay subsoils.

Our best advice is to always seek site specific advice in the first instance by reference to your local authority tree officer, or a qualified and experienced arboriculturalist, particularly if your neighbourhood is in a conservation area. By pruning regularly not only will the aesthetic shape of the tree be maintained but by restricting the leaf growth you will also restrict root spread and moisture demand. Always remember that even if your house is affected by tree growth desiccation, the degree of damage is usually very small and is more likely to be unsightly rather than structurally unsound. Preliminary research by the Building Research Establishment suggests:

- Detached properties have a greater susceptibility to subsidence or heave damage than non-detached properties.
- Properties built prior to 1900 are less susceptible to damage than those built thereafter.
- London clay is, by far, the most commonly encountered "problem" soil.
- It typically takes about 50 years between construction and perception of damage, while only about 6% of cases occurred in the first 10 years after construction.
- The likelihood of a property being underpinned following damage generally increases with the level of damage.
- Oak trees are, by far, the most damaging species of tree.

Avenue and street trees that are owned and maintained by the Local Authority have usually been chosen for their particular qualities: slower growing varieties requiring less maintenance or pruning are more appropriate to the street scene and have been fashionable for more than 50 years with the advent of the Town and Country Planning Act.

Before then developers and owners alike planted grand avenues of plane, poplar and elms. Alas many of the elms have succumbed to disease but the planes and poplars have now reached maturity. Plane especially can be cut back well without difficulty or serious harm to the tree. Most local authorities are aware of the relationship between trees and property and the risk of subsidence related damage that can occur.

The specific responsibility for the maintenance of the trees varies from authority to authority. If you think that a local authority tree is causing damage you should contact your authority's Tree Officer or Parks Department and seek their advice, but remember only if there are clear indications that damage is occurring. Suspicion that it may cause a problem is not sufficient. Some of the telltale signs to look for are:

- Diagonal cracks wider at one end than the other appearing in the walls around the doors and windows, both inside and out.

- Are the cracks wider than 5mm?
- Are any doors or windows sticking?
- Cracks around bay windows.
- Floors beginning to slope.

Isolated cracks in ceilings or at the junction of walls and ceilings are not likely to be indications of tree subsidence.

BENEFITS OF TREES

Most trees and shrubs in cities or communities are planted to provide beauty or shade. These are two excellent reasons for their use. Woody plants also serve many other purposes, and it often is helpful to consider these other functions when selecting a tree or shrub for the landscape. The benefits of trees can be grouped into social, communal, environmental, and economic categories.

Social Benefits

We like trees around us because they make life more pleasant. Most of us respond to the presence of trees beyond simply observing their beauty. We feel serene, peaceful, restful, and tranquil in a grove of trees. We are "at home" there. Hospital patients have been shown to recover from surgery more quickly when their hospital room offered a view of trees. The strong ties between people and trees are most evident in the resistance of community residents to removing trees to widen streets. Or we note the heroic efforts of individuals and organizations to save particularly large or historic trees in a community.

The stature, strength, and endurance of trees give them a cathedral-like quality. Because of their potential for long life, trees frequently are planted as living memorials. We often become personally attached to trees that we or those we love have planted.

Communal Benefits

Even though trees may be private property, their size often makes them part of the community as well. Because trees occupy considerable space, planning is required if both you and your neighbors are to benefit. With proper selection and maintenance, trees can enhance and function on one property without infringing on the rights and privileges of neighbours.

City trees often serve several architectural and engineering functions. They provide privacy, emphasize views, or screen out objectionable views. They reduce glare and reflection. They direct pedestrian traffic. They provide background to and soften, complement, or enhance architecture.

Environmental Benefits

Trees alter the environment in which we live by moderating climate, improving air quality, conserving water, and harboring wildlife. Climate control is obtained by moderating the effects of sun, wind, and rain. Radiant energy from the sun is absorbed or deflected by leaves on deciduous trees in the summer and is only filtered by branches of deciduous trees in winter. We are cooler when we stand in the shade of trees and are not exposed to direct sunlight. In winter, we value the sun's radiant energy. Therefore, we should plant only small or deciduous trees on the south side of homes.

Wind speed and direction can be affected by trees. The more compact the foliage on the tree or group of trees, the greater the influence of the windbreak. The downward fall of rain, sleet, and hail is initially absorbed or deflected by trees, which provides some protection for people, pets, and buildings. Trees intercept water, store some of it, and reduce storm runoff and the possibility of flooding.

Dew and frost are less common under trees because less radiant energy is released from the soil in those areas at night.

Temperature in the vicinity of trees is cooler than that away from trees. The larger the tree, the greater the cooling. By using trees in the cities, we are able to moderate the heat-island effect caused by pavement and buildings in commercial areas.

Air quality can be improved through the use of trees, shrubs, and turf. Leaves filter the air we breathe by removing dust and other particulates. Rain then washes the pollutants to the ground. Leaves absorb carbon dioxide from the air to form carbohydrates that are used in the plant's structure and function. In this process, leaves also absorb other air pollutants—such as ozone, carbon monoxide, and sulfur dioxide—and give off oxygen.

By planting trees and shrubs, we return to a more natural, less artificial environment. Birds and other wildlife are attracted to the area. The natural cycles of plant growth, reproduction, and decomposition are again present, both above and below ground. Natural harmony is restored to the urban environment.

Economic Benefits

Individual trees and shrubs have value, but the variability of species, size, condition, and function makes determining their economic value difficult. The economic benefits of trees can be both direct and indirect. Direct economic benefits are usually associated with energy costs. Air-conditioning costs are lower in a tree-shaded home. Heating costs are reduced when a home has a windbreak. Trees increase in value from the time they are planted until they mature. Trees are a wise investment of funds because landscaped homes are more valuable than nonlandscaped homes. The savings in energy costs and the increase in property value directly benefit each home owner.

The indirect economic benefits of trees are even greater. These benefits are available to the community or region. Lowered electricity bills are paid by customers when power companies are able to use less water in their cooling towers, build fewer new facilities to meet peak demands, use reduced amounts of fossil fuel in their furnaces, and use fewer measures to control air pollution. Communities also can save money if fewer facilities must be built to control storm water in the region. To the individual, these savings are small, but to the community, reductions in these expenses are often in the lakhs of rupees.

TREES REQUIRE AN INVESTMENT

Trees provide numerous aesthetic and economic benefits but also incur some costs. You need to be aware that an investment is required for your trees to provide the benefits that you desire. The biggest cost of trees and shrubs occurs when they are purchased and planted. Initial care almost always includes some watering. Leaf, branch, and whole tree removal and disposal can be expensive.

To function well in the landscape, trees require maintenance. Much can be done by the informed home owner. Corrective pruning and mulching gives trees a good start. Shade trees, however, quickly grow to a size that may require the services of a professional arborist. Arborists have the knowledge and equipment needed to prune, spray, fertilize, and otherwise maintain a large tree. Your garden center owner, university extension agent, community forester, or consulting arborist can answer questions about tree maintenance, suggest treatments, or recommend qualified arborists.

THE PHC ALTERNATIVE

Maintaining mature landscapes is a complicated undertaking. You may wish to consider a professional plant health care (PHC) maintenance programme that is now available from many landscape care companies. The programme is designed to maintain plant vigor and initially should include inspections to detect and treat any existing problems that could be damaging or fatal. Thereafter, regular inspections and preventive maintenance help ensure plant health and beauty. Refer to our plant health care brochure for more information.

TREE VALUES

This brochure is a home owner's guide to planning for, evaluating, and reducing possible financial losses on trees, specimen shrubs, and evergreens.

Almost everyone knows that trees and other living plants are valuable. They beautify our surroundings, purify our air, act as sound barriers, manufacture precious oxygen, and help us save energy through their cooling shade in summer and their wind reduction in winter. Many people don't realize, however, that plants have a dollar value of their own that can be measured by competent plant appraisers. If your trees or shrubs are damaged or destroyed, you may be able to recapture your loss through an insurance claim or as a deduction from your federal income tax.

Some Practical Advice

Here is some practical advice that may help you find out what your trees and plants are worth (a process known as valuation).

Planning for Highest Value

A professional in the tree, nursery, or landscape industry can help you plan, develop, install, and care for all of your trees and plants so that each of them will be worth more to you.

How Your Trees and Shrubs are Valuated

Seek the advice of professionals in this industry who have developed a set of guidelines for the valuation. Such guidelines have been widely adopted in the field and are recognized by insurance companies, the courts, and, in some cases, the Internal Revenue Service (IRS).

What to Do If You Suffer Loss or Damage to Your Landscape Plants

A casualty loss is defined by the IRS as "... a loss resulting from an identifiable event of sudden, unexpected, or unusual nature." This definition can include such events as vehicular accidents, storms, floods, lightning, vandalism, or even air and soil pollution.

If you suffer damage to trees or landscaping from any type of casualty, first consult your home owner's insurance policy to determine the amount and kind of coverage. Contact the insurance company to have an appraisal made by a competent tree and landscape professional who is experienced in plant appraisal. Have the appraisal made right after your loss or damage.

The tree and landscape appraiser accomplishes many things for you. The professional can see things you might miss, help correct damage, and prescribe remedies you may be able to do yourself. The appraiser will establish the amount of your loss in financial terms, including the cost of removing debris and making repairs as well as replacements. All of these steps are wise investments and well worth the cost you may incur for the inspection.

Four Factors in Professional Valuation of Trees and Other Plants

Size. Sometimes the size and age of a tree are such that it cannot be replaced. Trees that are too large to be replaced should be assessed by professionals who use a specialized appraisal formula.

Species or classification. Trees that are hardy, durable, highly adaptable, and free from objectionable characteristics are most valuable. They require less maintenance; they have sturdy, well-shaped branches, and pleasing foliage. Tree values vary according to your region, the "hardiness" zone, and even state and local conditions. If you are not familiar with these variables, be sure your advice comes from a competent source.

Condition. The professional will also consider the condition of the plant. Obviously, a healthy, well-maintained plant has a higher value. Roots, trunk, branches, and buds need to be inspected

Location. Functional considerations are important. A tree in your yard may be worth more than one growing in the woods. A tree standing alone often has a higher value than one in a group. A tree near your house or one that is a focal point in your landscape tends to have more value. The site, placement, and contribution of a tree to the overall landscape help determine the overall value of the plant attributable to location.

All of these factors can be measured in dollars and cents. They can determine the value of a tree, specimen shrubs, or evergreens, whether for insurance purposes, court testimony in lawsuits, or tax deductions.

CHECKLIST

These steps should be taken before and after any casualty loss to your trees and landscape. Taking them can improve the value of your investment in nature's green, growing gifts and prevent financial loss should they be damaged or destroyed.

- Plan your landscaping for both beauty and functional value.
- Protect and preserve to maintain value.

- Take pictures of trees and other landscape plants now while they are healthy and vigorous. Pictures make "before and after" comparisons easier and expedite the processing of insurance claims or deductions for losses on federal tax forms.
- Check your insurance. In most cases, the amount of an allowable claim for any one tree or shrub.
- For insurance, legal, and income tax purposes, keep accurate records of your landscape and real estate appraisals on any losses.
- Consult your local Plant Health Care professional at every stage in the life cycle of your landscape (planning, planting, care) and to make sure you do not suffer needless financial loss when a casualty strikes.

TREE SELECTION

Tree selection is one of the most important investment decisions a home owner makes when landscaping a new home or replacing a tree lost to damage or disease. Considering that most trees have the potential to outlive the people who plant them, the impact of this decision is one that can influence a lifetime. Match the tree to the site, and both lives will benefit.

The question most frequently asked of tree care professionals is "Which kind of tree do you think I should plant?" Before this question can be answered, a number of factors need to be considered. Think about the following questions:

- Why is the tree being planted? Do you want the tree to provide shade, fruit, or seasonal color, or act as a windbreak or screen? Maybe more than one reason?
- What is the size and location of the planting site? Does the space lend itself to a large, medium, or small tree? Are there overhead or belowground wires or utilities in the vicinity? Do you need to consider clearance for sidewalks, patios, or driveways? Are there other trees in the area? Are there barriers to future root growth, such as building foundations?

- Which type of soil conditions exist? Is the soil deep, fertile, and well drained, or is it shallow, compacted, and infertile?
- Which type of maintenance are you willing to provide? Do you have time to water, fertilize, and prune the newly planted tree until it is established, or will you be relying on your garden or tree service for assistance?

Asking and answering these and other questions before selecting a tree will help you choose the "right tree for the right place."

TREE FUNCTION

Trees make our surroundings more pleasant. Properly placed and cared for, trees increase the value of our real estate. A large shade tree provides relief from summer's heat and, when properly placed, can reduce summer cooling costs. An ornamental tree provides beautiful flowers, leaves, bark, or fruit. Evergreens with dense, persistent leaves can be used to provide a windbreak or a screen for privacy. A tree that drops its leaves in the fall allows the sun to warm a house in the winter. A tree or shrub that produces fruit can provide food for the owner and/or attract birds and wildlife into your home landscape. Street trees decrease the glare from pavement, reduce runoff, filter out pollutants, and add oxygen to the air we breath. Street trees also improve the overall appearance and quality of life in a city or neighborhood.

FORM AND SIZE

A basic principle of modern architecture is "form follows function." This is a good rule to remember when selecting a tree. Selecting the right form (shape) to complement the desired function (what you want the tree to do) can significantly reduce maintenance costs and increase the tree's value in the landscape. When making a selection about form, also consider mature tree size. Trees grow in a variety of sizes and shapes, as shown below. They can vary in height from several inches to several hundred feet. Select a form and size that will fit the planting space provided.

Depending on your site restrictions, you can choose from among hundreds of combinations of form and size. You may choose a small-spreading tree in a location with overhead utility lines. You may select a narrow, columnar form to provide a screen between two buildings. You may choose large, vase-shaped trees to create an arbor over a driveway or city street. You may even determine that the site just does not have enough space for a tree of any kind.

SITE CONDITIONS

Selecting a tree that will thrive in a given set of site conditions is the key to long-term tree survival. The following is a list of the major site conditions to consider before selecting a tree for planting:

- soil conditions;
- exposure (sun and wind);
- human activity;
- drainage;
- space constraints;
- hardiness zone.

SOIL CONDITIONS

The amount and quality of soil present in your yard can limit planting success. In urban sites, the topsoil often has been disturbed and frequently is shallow, compacted, and subject to drought. Under these conditions, trees are continuously under stress. For species that are not able to handle these types of conditions, proper maintenance designed to reduce stress is necessary to ensure adequate growth and survival. Many arborists will, for a minor charge, take soil samples from your yard to test for fertility, salinity, and pH (alkalinity or acidity). The tests will be returned with recommendations on ways to improve poor soil conditions with fertilizers or soil amendments (sand, compost, or manure) and will also help your local nursery or garden center recommend tree species that will do well in the soils found on your site.

Exposure

The amount of sunlight available will affect tree and shrub species selection for a particular location. Most woody plants require full sunlight for proper growth and flower bloom. Some do well in light shade, but few tree species perform well in dense shade. Exposure to wind is also a consideration. Wind can dry out soils, causing drought conditions and damage to branches and leaves during storms, and can actually uproot newly planted trees that have not had an opportunity to establish root systems. Special maintenance, such as staking or more frequent watering, may be needed to establish young trees on windy sites.

Human Activity

This aspect of tree selection is often overlooked. The reality of the situation is that the top five causes of tree death are the result of things people do: soil compaction, underwatering, overwatering, vandalism, and the number one cause—planting the wrong tree—account for more tree deaths than all insect and disease-related tree deaths combined.

Drainage

Tree roots require oxygen to develop and thrive. Poor drainage can remove the oxygen available to the roots from the soil and kill the tree. Before planting, dig some test holes 12 inches wide by 12 inches deep in the areas you are considering planting trees. Fill the holes with water and time how long it takes for the water to drain away. If it takes more than 6 hours, you may have a drainage problem. If so, ask your local garden center for recommendations on how to correct the problem, or choose a different site.

Space Constraints

Many different factors can limit the planting space available to the tree: overhead or underground utilities, pavement, buildings, other trees, visibility. The list goes on and on. Make sure there is adequate room for the tree you select to grow to maturity, both above and below ground.

Hardiness

Hardiness is the plant's ability to survive in the extreme temperatures of the particular geographic region in which you are planting the tree. Plants can be cold hardy, heat tolerant, or both. Most plant reference books provide a map of hardiness zone ranges. Although tropical areas are generally Zone 11, higher elevations have cooler temperatures that may warrant adjustment to the hardiness zone classification. Check with your local garden center for the hardiness information for your region. Before you make your final decision, make sure the plant you have selected is "hardy" in your area.

Pest Problems

Insect and disease organisms affect almost every tree and shrub species. Every plant has its particular pest problems, and the severity varies geographically. These pests may or may not be life threatening to the plant. You should select plants resistant to pest problems for your area. Your local ISA Certified Arborist, tree consultant, or extension agent can direct you to information relevant to problem species for your location.

Species Selection

Personal preferences play a major role in the selection process. Now that your homework is done, you are ready to select a species for the planting site you have chosen. Make sure you use the information you have gathered about your site conditions, and balance it with the aesthetic decisions you make related to your personal preferences.

The species must be suitable for the geographic region (hardy), tolerant to the moisture and drainage conditions of your soil, be resistant to pests in your area, and have the right form and size for the site and function you have envisioned.

Remember, the beautiful picture of a tree you looked at in a magazine or book was taken of a specimen that is growing vigorously because it was planted in the right place. If your site conditions tell you the species you selected will not do well under those conditions, do not be disappointed when the tree does not perform in the same way.

If you are having difficulty answering any of these questions on your own, contact a local ISA Certified Arborist, tree care professional, garden center, or extension agent for assistance. Their assistance will help you to plant the "right tree in the right place." It is better to get a professional involved early and help you make the right decision than to call him or her later to ask if you made the wrong decision.

This brochure is one in a series published by the International Society of Arboriculture as part of its Consumer Information Programme. You may have additional interest in the following titles currently in the series:

NEW TREE PLANTING

Think of the tree you just purchased as a lifetime investment. How well your tree, and investment, grows depends on the type of tree and location you select for planting, the care you provide when the tree is planted, and follow-up care the tree receives after planting.

Planting the Tree

The ideal time to plant trees and shrubs is during the dormant season'Äîin the fall after leaf drop or early spring before budbreak. Weather conditions are cool and allow plants to establish roots in the new location before spring rains and summer heat stimulate new top growth. However, trees properly cared for in the nursery or garden center, and given the appropriate care during transport to prevent damage, can be planted throughout the growing season. In tropical and subtropical climates where trees grow year round, any time is a good time to plant a tree, provided that sufficient water is available. In either situation, proper handling during planting is essential to ensure a healthy future for new trees and shrubs. Before you begin planting your tree, be sure you have had all underground utilities located prior to digging.

If the tree you are planting is balled or bare root, it is important to understand that its root system has been reduced by 90 to 95 per cent of its original size during transplanting. As a result of the trauma caused by the digging process, trees commonly exhibit what is known as transplant shock. Containerized trees may also experience transplant shock, particularly if they have circling roots that must be cut. Transplant shock is indicated by slow growth and reduced vigor following transplanting. Proper site preparation before and during planting coupled with good follow-up care reduces the amount of time the plant experiences transplant shock and allows the tree to quickly establish in its new location. Carefully follow ten simple steps, and you can significantly reduce the stress placed on the plant at the time of planting:

- Dig a shallow, broad planting hole. Make the hole wide, as much as three times the diameter of the root ball but only as deep as the root ball. It is important to make the hole wide because the roots on the newly establishing tree must push through surrounding soil in order to establish. On most planting sites in new developments, the existing soils have been compacted and are unsuitable for healthy root growth. Breaking up the soil in a large area around the tree provides the newly emerging roots room to expand into loose soil to hasten establishment.

- Identify the trunk flare. The trunk flare is where the roots spread at the base of the tree. This point should be partially visible after the tree has been planted. If the trunk flare is not partially visible, you may have to remove some soil from the top of the root ball. Find it so you can determine how deep the hole needs to be for proper planting.

- Remove tree container for containerized trees. Carefully cutting down the sides of the container may make this easier. Inspect the root ball for circling roots and cut or remove them. Expose the trunk flare, if necessary.

- Place the tree at the proper height. Before placing the tree in the hole, check to see that the hole has been dug to the proper depth'. The majority of the roots on the newly planted tree will develop in the top 12 inches of soil. If the tree is planted too deeply, new roots will have difficulty developing because of a lack of oxygen. It is better to plant the tree a little high, 2 to 3 inches above the base of the trunk flare, than to plant it at or below the original growing level. This planting level will allow for some settling. To avoid damage when setting the tree in the hole, always lift the tree by the root ball and never by the trunk.

- Straighten the tree in the hole. Before you begin backfilling, have someone view the tree from several directions to confirm that the tree is straight. Once you begin backfilling, it is difficult to reposition the tree.
- Fill the hole gently but firmly. Fill the hole about one-third full and gently but firmly pack the soil around the base of the root ball. Then, if the root ball is wrapped, cut and remove any fabric, plastic, string, and wire from around the trunk and root ball to facilitate growth. Be careful not to damage the trunk or roots in the process.
- Stake the tree, if necessary. If the tree is grown and dug properly at the nursery, staking for support will not be necessary in most home landscape situations. Studies have shown that trees establish more quickly and develop stronger trunk and root systems if they are not staked at the time of planting. However, protective staking may be required on sites where lawn mower damage, vandalism, or windy conditions are concerns. If staking is necessary for support, there are three methods to choose among: staking, guying, and ball stabilizing. One of the most common methods is staking. With this method, two stakes used in conjunction with a wide, flexible tie material on the lower half of the tree will hold the tree upright, provide flexibility, and minimize injury to the trunk. Remove support staking and ties after the first year of growth.
- Mulch the base of the tree. Mulch is simply organic matter applied to the area at the base of the tree. It acts as a blanket to hold moisture, it moderates soil temperature extremes, and it reduces competition from grass and weeds. Some good choices are leaf litter, pine straw, shredded bark, peat moss, or composted wood chips. A 2- to 4-inch layer is ideal. More than 4 inches may cause a problem with oxygen and moisture levels. When placing mulch, be sure that the actual

trunk of the tree is not covered. Doing so may cause decay of the living bark at the base of the tree. A mulch-free area, 1 to 2 inches wide at the base of the tree, is sufficient to avoid moist bark conditions and prevent decay.

- Provide follow-up care. Keep the soil moist but not soaked; overwatering causes leaves to turn yellow or fall off. Water trees at least once a week, barring rain, and more frequently during hot weather. When the soil is dry below the surface of the mulch, it is time to water. Continue until mid-fall, tapering off for lower temperatures that require less-frequent watering.
- Other follow-up care may include minor pruning of branches damaged during the planting process. Prune sparingly immediately after planting and wait to begin necessary corrective pruning until after a full season of growth in the new location.

After you'have completed these ten simple steps mentioned above, further routine care and favorable weather conditions will ensure that your new tree or shrub will grow and thrive. A valuable asset to any landscape, trees provide a long-lasting source of beauty and enjoyment for people of all ages. When questions arise about the care of your tree, be sure to consult your local ISA Certified Arborist or a tree care or garden center professional for assistance.

Maintaining mature landscapes is a complicated undertaking. You may wish to consider a professional Plant Health Care (PHC) maintenance programme, which is now available from many landscape care companies. A PHC programme is designed to maintain plant vigour and should initially include inspections to detect and treat any existing problems that could be damaging or fatal. Thereafter, regular inspections and preventive maintenance will ensure plant health and beauty.

MATURE TREE CARE

Think of tree care as an investment. A healthy tree increases in value with age—paying big dividends, increasing property values, beautifying our surroundings, purifying our air, and saving energy by providing cooling shade from summer's heat and protection from winter's wind.

Providing a preventive care programme for your landscape plants is like putting money in the bank. Regular maintenance, designed to promote plant health and vigor, ensures their value will continue to grow. Preventing a problem is much less costly and time-consuming than curing one once it has developed. An effective maintenance programme, including regular inspections and the necessary follow-up care of mulching, fertilizing, and pruning, can detect problems and correct them before they become damaging or fatal. Considering that many tree species can live as long as 200 to 300 years, including these practices when caring for your home landscape is an investment that will offer enjoyment and value for generations.

Tree Inspection

Tree inspection is an evaluation tool to call attention to any change in the tree's health before the problem becomes too serious. By providing regular inspections of mature trees at least once a year, you can prevent or reduce the severity of future disease, insect, and environmental problems. During tree inspection, be sure to examine four characteristics of tree vigor: new leaves or buds, leaf size, twig growth, and absence of crown dieback (gradual death of the upper part of the tree).

A reduction in the extension of shoots (new growing parts), such as buds or new leaves, is a fairly reliable cue that the tree's health has recently changed. To evaluate this factor, compare the growth of the shoots over the past three years. Determine whether there is a reduction in the tree's typical growth pattern.

Further signs of poor tree health are trunk decay, crown dieback, or both. These symptoms often indicate problems that began several years before. Loose bark or deformed growths, such as trunk conks (mushrooms), are common signs of stem decay.

Any abnormalities found during these inspections, including insect activity and spotted, deformed, discolored, or dead leaves and twigs, should be noted and watched closely. If you are uncertain as to what should be done, report your findings to your local ISA Certified Arborist or other tree care professional for advice on possible treatment.

Mulching

Mulching can reduce environmental stress by providing trees with a stable root environment that is cooler and contains more moisture than the surrounding soil. Mulch can also prevent mechanical damage by keeping machines such as lawn mowers and string trimmers away from the tree's base. Further, mulch reduces competition from surrounding weeds and turf.

To be most effective in all of these functions, mulch should be placed 2 to 4 inches deep and cover the entire root system, which may be as far as 2 or 3 times the diameter of the branch spread of the tree. If the area and activities happening around the tree do not permit the entire area to be mulched, it is recommended that you mulch as much of the area under the drip line of the tree as possible. When placing mulch, care should be taken not to cover the actual trunk of the tree. This mulch-free area, 1 to 2 inches wide at the base, is sufficient to avoid moist bark conditions and prevent trunk decay.

An organic mulch layer 2 to 4 inches deep of loosely packed shredded leaves, pine straw, peat moss, or composted wood chips is adequate. Plastic should not be used because it interferes with the exchange of gases between soil and air, which inhibits root growth. Thicker mulch layers, 5 to 6 inches deep or greater, may also inhibit gas exchange.

Fertilization

Fertilization is another important aspect of mature tree care. Trees require certain nutrients (essential elements) to function and grow. Urban landscape trees can be growing in soils that do not contain sufficient available nutrients for satisfactory growth and development. In these situations, it may be necessary to fertilize to improve plant vigor.

Fertilizing a tree can improve growth; however, if fertilizer is not applied wisely, it may not benefit the tree at all and may even adversely affect the tree. Mature trees making satisfactory growth may not require fertilization. When considering supplemental fertilizer, it is important to know which nutrients are needed and when and how they should be applied.

Soil conditions, especially pH and organic matter content, vary greatly, making the proper selection and use of fertilizer a somewhat complex process. When dealing with a mature tree that provides considerable benefit and value to your landscape, it is worth the time and investment to have the soil tested for nutrient content. Any arborist can arrange to have your soil tested at a soil testing laboratory and can give advice on application rates, timing, and the best blend of fertilizer for each of your trees and other landscape plants.

Mature trees have expansive root systems that extend from 2 to 3 times the size of the leaf canopy. A major portion of actively growing roots is located outside the tree's drip line. It is important to understand this fact when applying fertilizer to your trees as well as your turf. Many lawn fertilizers contain weed and feed formulations that may be harmful to your trees. When you apply a broadleaf herbicide to your turf, remember that tree roots coexist with turf roots. The same herbicide that kills broadleaf weeds in your lawn is picked up by tree roots and can harm or kill your broadleaf trees if applied incorrectly. Understanding the actual size and extent of a tree's root system before you fertilize is necessary to determine how much, what type, and where to best apply fertilizer.

Pruning

Pruning is the most common tree maintenance procedure next to watering. Pruning is often desirable or necessary to remove dead, diseased, or insect-infested branches and to improve tree structure, enhance vigor, or maintain safety. Because each cut has the potential to change the growth of (or cause damage to) a tree, no branch should be removed without a reason.

Removing foliage from a tree has two distinct effects on its growth. Removing leaves reduces photosynthesis and may reduce overall growth. That is why pruning should always be performed sparingly. Overpruning is extremely harmful because without enough leaves, a tree cannot gather and process enough sunlight to survive. However, after pruning, the growth that does occur takes place on fewer shoots, so they tend to grow longer than they would without pruning. Understanding how the tree responds to pruning should assist you when selecting branches for removal.

Pruning mature trees may require special equipment, training, and experience. If the pruning work requires climbing, the use of a chain or hand saw, or the removal of large limbs, then using personal safety equipment, such as protective eyewear and hearing protection, is a must. Arborists can provide a variety of services to assist in performing the job safely and reducing risk of personal injury and damage to your property. They also are able to determine which type of pruning is necessary to maintain or improve the health, appearance, and safety of your trees.

Although tree removal is a last resort, there are circumstances when it is necessary. An arborist can help decide whether or not a tree should be removed. Professionally trained arborists have the skills and equipment to safely and efficiently remove trees. Removal is recommended when a tree:

- is dead, dying, or considered irreparably hazardous;
- is causing an obstruction or is crowding and causing harm to other trees and the situation is impossible to correct through pruning;
- is to be replaced by a more suitable specimen;
- should be removed to allow for construction.

With proper maintenance, trees are attractive and can add considerable value to your property. Poorly maintained trees, on the other hand, can be a significant liability. Pruning or removing trees, especially large trees, can be dangerous work. It should be performed only by those trained and equipped to work safely in trees. For more information on mature tree care, contact your local ISA Certified Arborist.

Maintaining mature landscapes is a complicated undertaking. You may wish to consider a professional Plant

Health Care maintenance programme, which is now available from many landscape care companies. A PHC programme is designed to maintain plant vigor and should initially include inspections to detect and treat any existing problems that could be damaging or fatal. Thereafter, regular inspections and preventive maintenance will ensure plant health and beauty. Refer to our Plant Health Care brochure for more information.

Pruning of Young Trees

Proper pruning is essential in developing a tree with a strong structure and desirable form. Trees that receive the appropriate pruning measures while they are young will require little corrective pruning when they mature.

Keep these few simple principles in mind before pruning a tree:

- Each cut has the potential to change the growth of the tree. Always have a purpose in mind before making a cut.
- Proper technique is essential. Poor pruning can cause damage that lasts for the life of the tree. Learn where and how to make the cuts before picking up the pruning shears.
- Trees do not heal the way people do. When a tree is wounded, it must grow over and compartmentalize the wound. As a result, the wound is contained within the tree forever.
- Small cuts do less damage to the tree than large cuts. For that reason, proper pruning (training) of young trees is critical. Waiting to prune a tree until it is mature can create the need for large cuts that the tree cannot easily close.

Making the Cut

Where you make a pruning cut is critical to a tree's response in growth and wound closure. Make pruning cuts just outside the branch collar. Because the branch collar contains trunk or parent branch tissues, the tree will be damaged unnecessarily if you remove or damage it. In fact, if the cut is large, the tree may suffer permanent internal decay from an improper pruning cut.

If a permanent branch is to be shortened, cut it back to a lateral branch or bud. Internodal cuts, or cuts made between buds or branches, may lead to stem decay, sprout production, and misdirected growth.

Pruning Tools

When pruning trees, it is important to have the right tool for the job. For small trees, most of the cuts can be made with hand pruning shears (secateurs). The scissor-type, or bypass blade hand pruners, are preferred over the anvil type. They make cleaner, more accurate cuts. Cuts larger than one-half inch in diameter should be made with lopping shears or a pruning saw.

Never use hedge shears to prune a tree. Whatever tool you use, make sure it is kept clean and sharp.

Establishing a Strong Scaffold Structure

A good structure of primary scaffold branches should be established while the tree is young. The scaffold branches provide the framework of the mature tree. Properly trained young trees will develop a strong structure that requires less corrective pruning as they mature.

The goal in training young trees is to establish a strong trunk with sturdy, well-spaced branches. The strength of the branch structure depends on the relative sizes of the branches, the branch angles, and the spacing of the limbs. Naturally, those factors vary with the growth habit of the tree. Pin oaks and sweetgums, for example, have a conical shape with a central leader. Elms and live oaks are often wide-spreading without a central leader. Other trees, such as lindens and Bradford pears, are densely branched. Good pruning techniques remove structurally weak branches while maintaining the natural form of the tree.

Trunk Development

For most young trees, maintain a single dominant leader growing upward. Do not prune back the tip of this leader. Do not allow secondary branches to outgrow the leader. Sometimes a tree will develop double leaders known as co-dominant stems.

Co-dominant stems can lead to structural weaknesses, so it is best to remove one of the stems while the tree is young.

The lateral branches growing on the sides contribute to the development of a sturdy well-tapered trunk. It is important to leave some of these lateral branches in place, even though they may be pruned out later. These branches, known as temporary branches, also help protect the trunk from sun and mechanical injury. Temporary branches should be kept short enough not to be an obstruction or compete with selected permanent branches.

Permanent Branch Selection

Nursery trees often have low branches that may make the tree appear well-proportioned when young, but low branches are seldom appropriate for large-growing trees in an urban environment. How a young tree is trained depends on its primary function in the landscape. For example, street trees must be pruned so that they allow at least 16 feet of clearance for traffic. Most landscape trees require only about 8 feet of clearance.

The height of the lowest permanent branch is determined by the tree's intended function and location in the landscape. Trees that are used to screen an unsightly view or provide a wind break may be allowed to branch low to the ground. Most large-growing trees in the landscape must eventually be pruned to allow head clearance.

The spacing of branches, both vertically and radially, in the tree is very important. Branches selected as permanent scaffold branches must be well-spaced along the trunk. Maintain radial balance with branches growing outward in each direction.

A good rule of thumb for the vertical spacing of permanent branches is to maintain a distance equal to 3 percent of the tree's eventual height. Thus, a tree that will be 50 feet tall should have permanent scaffold branches spaced about 18 inches apart along the trunk. Avoid allowing two scaffold branches to arise one above the other on the same side of the tree.

Some trees have a tendency to develop branches with narrow angles of attachment and tight crotches. As the tree grows, bark can become enclosed deep within the crotch between the branch and the trunk. Such growth is called included bark. Included bark weakens the attachment of the branch to the trunk and can lead to branch failure when the tree matures. You should prune branches with weak attachments while they are young.

Avoid overthinning the interior of the tree. The leaves of each branch must manufacture enough food to keep that branch alive and growing. In addition, each branch must contribute food to grow and feed the trunk and roots. Removal of too many leaves can "starve" the tree, reduce growth, and make the tree unhealthy. A good rule of thumb is to maintain at least half the foliage on branches arising in the lower two-thirds of the tree.

Newly Planted Trees

Pruning of newly planted trees should be limited to corrective pruning. Remove torn or broken branches, and save other pruning measures for the second or third year.

The belief that trees should be pruned when planted to compensate for root loss is misguided. Trees need their leaves and shoot tips to provide food and the substances that stimulate new root production. Unpruned trees establish faster with a stronger root system than trees pruned at the time of planting.

Wound Dressings

Wound dressings were once thought to accelerate wound closure, protect against insects and diseases, and reduce decay.

However, research has shown that dressings do not reduce decay or speed closure and rarely prevent insect or disease infestations. Most experts recommend that wound dressing not be used. If a dressing must be used for cosmetic purposes, use a thin coating of a material that is not toxic to the plant.

This brochure is one in a series published by the International Society of Arboriculture as part of its Consumer Information Programme. You may have additional interest in the following titles currently in the series:

For most young trees, maintain a single dominant leader growing upward. Do not prune back the tip of this leader. Do not allow secondary branches to outgrow the leader. Sometimes a tree will develop double leaders known as co-dominant stems. Co-dominant stems can lead to structural weaknesses, so it is best to remove one of the stems while the tree is young.

The lateral branches growing on the sides contribute to the development of a sturdy well-tapered trunk. It is important to leave some of these lateral branches in place, even though they may be pruned out later. These branches, known as temporary branches, also help protect the trunk from sun and mechanical injury. Temporary branches should be kept short enough not to be an obstruction or compete with selected permanent branches.

Permanent Branch Selection

Nursery trees often have low branches that may make the tree appear well-proportioned when young, but low branches are seldom appropriate for large-growing trees in an urban environment. How a young tree is trained depends on its primary function in the landscape. For example, street trees must be pruned so that they allow at least 16 feet of clearance for traffic. Most landscape trees require only about 8 feet of clearance.

The height of the lowest permanent branch is determined by the tree's intended function and location in the landscape. Trees that are used to screen an unsightly view or provide a wind break may be allowed to branch low to the ground. Most large-growing trees in the landscape must eventually be pruned to allow head clearance.

The spacing of branches, both vertically and radially, in the tree is very important. Branches selected as permanent scaffold branches must be well-spaced along the trunk. Maintain radial balance with branches growing outward in each direction.

A good rule of thumb for the vertical spacing of permanent branches is to maintain a distance equal to 3 percent of the tree's eventual height. Thus, a tree that will be 50 feet tall should have permanent scaffold branches spaced about 18 inches apart along the trunk. Avoid allowing two scaffold branches to arise one above the other on the same side of the tree.

Some trees have a tendency to develop branches with narrow angles of attachment and tight crotches. As the tree grows, bark can become enclosed deep within the crotch between the branch and the trunk. Such growth is called included bark. Included bark weakens the attachment of the branch to the trunk and can lead to branch failure when the tree matures. You should prune branches with weak attachments while they are young.

Avoid overthinning the interior of the tree. The leaves of each branch must manufacture enough food to keep that branch alive and growing. In addition, each branch must contribute food to grow and feed the trunk and roots. Removal of too many leaves can "starve" the tree, reduce growth, and make the tree unhealthy. A good rule of thumb is to maintain at least half the foliage on branches arising in the lower two-thirds of the tree.

Newly Planted Trees

Pruning of newly planted trees should be limited to corrective pruning. Remove torn or broken branches, and save other pruning measures for the second or third year.

The belief that trees should be pruned when planted to compensate for root loss is misguided. Trees need their leaves and shoot tips to provide food and the substances that stimulate new root production. Unpruned trees establish faster with a stronger root system than trees pruned at the time of planting.

Wound Dressings

Wound dressings were once thought to accelerate wound closure, protect against insects and diseases, and reduce decay. However, research has shown that dressings do not reduce decay or speed closure and rarely prevent insect or disease infestations. Most experts recommend that wound dressing not be used. If a dressing must be used for cosmetic purposes, use a thin coating of a material that is not toxic to the plant.

This brochure is one in a series published by the International Society of Arboriculture as part of its Consumer Information Programme.

CHAPTER 3

Pruning of Trees

INTRODUCTION

The objective of pruning is to produce strong, healthy, attractive plants. By understanding how, when and why to prune, and by following a few simple principles, this objective can be achieved.

The main reasons for pruning ornamental and shade trees include safety, health, and aesthetics. In addition, pruning can be used to stimulate fruit production and increase the value of timber. Pruning for *safety* involves removing branches that could fall and cause injury or property damage, trimming branches that interfere with lines of sight on streets or driveways, and removing branches that grow into utility lines. Safety pruning can be largely avoided by carefully choosing species that will not grow beyond the space available to them, and have strength and form characteristics that are suited to the site.

Pruning for *health* involves removing diseased or insect-infested wood, thinning the crown to increase airflow and reduce some pest problems, and removing crossing and rubbing branches. Pruning can best be used to encourage trees to develop a strong structure and reduce the likelihood of damage during severe weather. Removing broken or damaged limbs encourages wound closure.

Pruning for *aesthetics* involves enhancing the natural form and character of trees or stimulating flower production. Pruning for form can be especially important on open-grown trees that do very little self-pruning.

All woody plants shed branches in response to shading and competition. Branches that do not produce enough carbohydrates from photosynthesis to sustain themselves die and are eventually shed; the resulting wounds are sealed by woundwood (callus). Branches that are poorly attached may be broken off by wind and accumulation of snow and ice. Branches removed by such natural forces often result in large, ragged wounds that rarely seal. Pruning as a cultural practice can be used to supplement or replace these natural processes and increase the strength and longevity of plants.

Trees have many forms, but the most common types are pyramidal (excurrent) or spherical (decurrent). Trees with pyramidal crowns, e.g., most conifers, have a strong central stem and lateral branches that are more or less horizontal and do not compete with the central stem for dominance. Trees with spherical crowns, e.g., most hardwoods, have many lateral branches that may compete for dominance.

To reduce the need for pruning it is best to consider a tree's natural form. It is very difficult to impose an unnatural form on a tree without a commitment to constant maintenance.

Pollarding and topiary are extreme examples of pruning to create a desired, unnatural effect. Pollarding is the practice of pruning trees annually to remove all new growth. The following year, a profusion of new branches is produced at the ends of the branches. Topiary involves pruning trees and shrubs into geometric or animal shapes. Both pollarding and topiary are specialized applications that involve pruning to change the natural form of trees. As topiary demonstrates, given enough care and attention, plants can be pruned into nearly any form. Yet just as proper pruning can enhance the form or character of plants, improper pruning can destroy it.

PRUNING APPROACHES

Producing strong structure should be the emphasis when pruning young trees. As trees mature, the aim of pruning will shift to maintaining tree structure, form, health and appearance.

Proper pruning cuts are made at a node, the point at which one branch or twig attaches to another. In the spring of the year growth begins at buds, and twigs grow until a new node is formed. The length of a branch between nodes is called an internode.

The most common types of pruning are:

1. *Crown thinning*– Primarily for hardwoods, is the selective removal of branches to increase light penetration and air movement throughout the crown of a tree. The intent is to maintain or develop a tree's structure and form. To avoid unnecessary stress and prevent excessive production of epicormic sprouts, no more than one-quarter of the living crown should be removed at a time. If it is necessary to remove more, it should be done over successive years.

   Branches with strong U-shaped angles of attachment should be retained. Branches with narrow, V-shaped angles of attachment often form included bark and should be removed. Included bark forms when two branches grow at sharply acute angles to one another, producing a wedge of inward-rolled bark between them. Included bark prevents strong attachment of branches, often causing a crack at the point below where the branches meet. Codominant stems that are approximately the same size and arise from the same position often form included bark. Removing some of the lateral branches from a codominant stem can reduce its growth enough to allow the other stem to become dominant.

   Lateral branches should be no more than one-half to three-quarters of the diameter of the stem at the point of attachment. Avoid producing "lion's tails", tufts of branches and foliage at the ends of branches, caused by removing all inner lateral branches and foliage. Lion's tails can result in sunscalding, abundant epicormic sprouts, and weak branch structure and breakage. Branches that rub or cross another branch should be removed.

Conifers that have branches in whorls and pyramidal crowns rarely need crown thinning except to restore a dominant leader. Occasionally, the leader of a tree may be damaged and multiple branches may become codominant. Select the strongest leader and remove competing branches to prevent the development of codominant stems.

Assess how a tree will be pruned from the top down.

Favour branches with strong, U-shaped angles of attachment. Remove branches with weak, V-shaped angles of attachment and/or included bark.

Ideally, lateral branches should be evenly spaced on the main stem of young trees.

Remove any branches that rub or cross another branch.

Make sure that lateral branches are no more than one-half to three-quarters of the diameter of the stem to discourage the development of co-dominant stems.

Do not remove more than one- quarter of the living crown of a tree at one time. If it is necessary to remove more, do it over successive years.

2. *Crown Raising*– Crown raising is the practice of removing branches from the bottom of the crown of a tree to provide clearance for pedestrians, vehicles, buildings, lines of site, or to develop a clear stem for timber production. Also, removing lower branches on white pines can prevent blister rust. For street trees the minimum clearance is often specified by municipal ordinance. After pruning, the ratio of the living crown to total tree height should be at least two-thirds (e.g., a 12 m tree should have living branches on at least the upper 8 m).

   On young trees "temporary" branches may be retained along the stem to encourage taper and protect trees from vandalism and sun scald. Less vigorous shoots should be selected as temporary branches and should be about 10 to 15 cm apart along the stem. They should be pruned annually to slow their growth and should be removed eventually.

Always maintain live branches on at least two-thirds of a tree's total height. Removing too many lower branches will hinder the development of a strong stem.

Remove basal sprouts and vigorous epicormic sprouts.

3. ***Crown Reduction***– Crown reduction pruning is most often used when a tree has grown too large for its permitted space. This method, sometimes called drop crotch pruning, is preferred to topping because it results in a more natural appearance, increases the time before pruning is needed again, and minimizes stress (see drop crotch cuts in the next section).

   Crown reduction pruning, a method of last resort, often results in large pruning wounds to stems that may lead to decay. This method should never be used on a tree with a pyramidal growth form. A better long term solution is to remove the tree and replace it with a tree that will not grow beyond the available space.

   Use crown reduction pruning only when absolutely necessary. Make the pruning cut at a lateral branch that is at least one-third the diameter of the stem to be removed.

   If it is necessary to remove more than half of the foliage from a branch, remove the entire branch.

PRUNING CUTS

Pruning cuts should be made so that only branch tissue is removed and stem tissue is not damaged. At the point where the branch attaches to the stem, branch and stem tissues remain separate, but are contiguous. If only branch tissues are cut when pruning, the stem tissues of the tree will probably not become decayed, and the wound will seal more effectively.

1. Pruning living branches

To find the proper place to cut a branch, look for the branch collar that grows from the stem tissue at the underside of the base of the branch. On the upper surface, there is usually a branch bark ridge that runs (more or less) parallel to the branch angle, along the stem of the tree. A proper pruning cut does not damage either the branch bark ridge or the branch collar.

A proper cut begins just outside the branch bark ridge and angles down away from the stem of the tree, avoiding injury to the branch collar . Make the cut as close as possible to the stem in the branch axil, but outside the branch bark ridge, so that stem tissue is not injured and the wound can seal in the shortest time possible. If the cut is too far from the stem, leaving a branch stub, the branch tissue usually dies and woundwood forms from the stem tissue. Wound closure is delayed because the woundwood must seal over the stub that was left.

The quality of pruning cuts can be evaluated by examining pruning wounds after one growing season. A concentric ring of woundwood will form from proper pruning cuts . Flush cuts made inside the branch bark ridge or branch collar, result in pronounced development of woundwood on the sides of the pruning wounds with very little woundwood forming on the top or bottom). As described above, stub cuts result in the death of the remaining branch and woundwood forms around the base from stem tissues.

When pruning small branches with hand pruners, make sure the tools are sharp enough to cut the branches cleanly without tearing. Branches large enough to require saws should be supported with one hand while the cuts are made. If the branch is too large to support, make a three-step pruning cut to prevent bark ripping.

1. The first cut is a shallow notch made on the underside of the branch, outside the branch collar. This cut will prevent a falling branch from tearing the stem tissue as it pulls away from the tree.

2. The second cut should be outside the first cut, all the way through the branch, leaving a short stub.

3. The stub is then cut just outside the branch bark ridge/ branch collar, completing the operation.

2. Pruning Dead Branches

Prune dead branches in much the same way as live branches. Making the correct cut is usually easy because the branch collar and the branch bark ridge can be distinguished from the dead branch because they continue to grow Make the pruning cut just outside of the ring of woundwood tissue that has formed, being careful not to cause unnecessary injury Large dead branches should be supported with one hand or cut with the three-step method, just as live branches. Cutting large living branches with the three step method is more critical because of the greater likelihood of bark ripping.

3. Drop Crotch Cuts

A proper cut begins just above the branch bark ridge and extends through the stem parallel to the branch bark ridge. Usually, the stem being removed is too large to be supported with one hand, so the three cut method should be used.

With the first cut, make a notch on the side of the stem away from the branch to be retained, well above the branch crotch.

1. Begin the second cut inside the branch crotch, staying well above the branch bark ridge, and cut through the stem above the notch.

2. Cut the remaining stub just inside the branch bark ridge through the stem parallel to the branch bark ridge.

To prevent the abundant growth of epicormic sprouts on the stem below the cut, or dieback of the stem to a lower lateral branch, make the cut at a lateral branch that is at least one-third of the diameter of the stem at their union.

WHEN TO PRUNE

Conifers may be pruned any time of the year, but pruning during the dormant season may minimize sap and resin flow from cut branches.

Hardwood trees and shrubs without showy flowers: Prune in the dormant season to easily visualize the structure of the tree, to maximize wound closure in the growing season after pruning, to reduce the chance of transmitting disease, and to discourage excessive sap flow from wounds. Recent wounds and the chemical scents they emit can actually attract insects that spread tree disease. In particular, wounded elm wood is known to attract bark beetles that harbor spores of the Dutch elm disease fungus, and open wounds on oaks are known to attract beetles that spread the oak wilt fungus. Take care to prune these trees during the correct time of year to prevent spread of these fatal diseases. Contact your local tree disease specialist to find out when to prune these tree species in your area. Usually, the best time is during the late fall and winter.

Flowering trees and shrubs: These should also be pruned during the dormant season for the same reasons stated above; however, to preserve the current year's flower crop, prune according to the following schedule:

- Trees and shrubs that flower in early spring (redbud, dogwood, etc.) should be pruned immediately after flowering (flower buds arise the year before they flush, and will form on the new growth).
- Many flowering trees are susceptible to fireblight, a bacterial disease that can be spread by pruning. These trees, including many varieties of crabapple, hawthorn, pear, mountain ash, flowering quince and pyracantha, should be pruned during the dormant season. Check with your county extension agent or a horticulturist for additional information.
- Trees and shrubs that flower in the summer or fall always should be pruned during the dormant season (flower buds will form on new twigs during the next growing season, and the flowers will flush normally).
- *Dead branches:* can be removed any time of the year.

Pruning Tools– Proper tools are essential for satisfactory pruning . The choice of which tool to use depends largely on the size of branches to be pruned and the amount of pruning to be done. If possible, test a tool before you buy it to ensure it suits your specific needs. As with most things, higher quality often equates to higher cost.

Generally speaking, the smaller a branch is when pruned, the sooner the wound created will seal. Hand pruners are used to prune small branches (under 2.5 cm diameter) and many different kinds are available. Hand pruners can be grouped into by-pass or anvil styles based on the blade configuration. Anvil style pruners have a straight blade that cuts the branch against a small anvil or block as the handles are squeezed. By-pass pruners use a curved cutting blade that slides past a broader lower blade, much like a scissors. To prevent unnecessary tearing or crushing of tissues, it is best to use a by-pass style pruner. Left- or right-handed types can be purchased.

Slightly larger branches that cannot be cut with a hand pruner may be cut with small pruning saws (up to 10 cm) or lopping shears (up to 7 cm diameter) with larger cutting surfaces and greater leverage. Lopping shears are also available in by-pass and anvil styles.

For branches too large to be cut with a hand pruner or lopping shears, pruning saws must be used. Pruning saws differ greatly in handle styles, the length and shape of the blade, and the layout and type of teeth. Most have tempered metal blades that retain their sharpness for many pruning cuts. Unlike most other saws, pruning saws are often designed to cut on the "pull-stroke."

Chain saws are preferred when pruning branches larger than about 10 cm. Chainsaws should be used only by qualified individuals. To avoid the need to cut branches greater than 10 cm diameter, prune when branches are small.

Pole pruners must be used to cut branches beyond reach. Generally, pruning heads can cut branches up to 4.4 cm diameter and are available in the by-pass and anvil styles. Once again, the by-pass type is preferred. For cutting larger branches, saw blades can be fastened directly to the pruning head, or a separate saw head can be purchased. Because of the danger of electrocution, pole pruners should not be used near utility lines except by qualified utility line clearance personnel.

To ensure that satisfactory cuts are made and to reduce fatigue, keep your pruning tools sharp and in good working condition. Hand pruners, lopping shears, and pole pruners should be periodically sharpened with a sharpening stone. Replacement blades are available for many styles. Pruning saws should be professionally sharpened or periodically replaced. To reduce cost, many styles have replaceable blades.

Tools should be clean and sanitized as well as sharp. Although sanitizing tools may be inconvenient and seldom practiced, doing so may prevent the spread of disease from infected to healthy trees on contaminated tools. Tools become contaminated when they come into contact with fungi, bacteria, viruses and other microorganisms that cause disease in trees. Most pathogens need some way of entering the tree to cause disease, and fresh wounds are perfect places for infections to begin. Microorganisms on tool surfaces are easily introduced into susceptible trees when subsequent cuts are made. The need for sanitizing tools can be greatly reduced by pruning during the dormant season.

If sanitizing is necessary it should be practiced as follows: Before each branch is cut, sanitize pruning tools with either 70% denatured alcohol, or with liquid household bleach diluted 1 to 9 with water (1 part bleach, 9 parts water). Tools should be immersed in the solution, preferably for 1-2 minutes, and wood particles should be wiped from all cutting surfaces. Bleach is corrosive to metal surfaces, so tools should be thoroughly cleaned with soap and water after each use.

Treating Wounds Tree sap, gums, and resins are the natural means by which trees combat invasion by pathogens. Although unsightly, sap flow from pruning wounds is not generally harmful; however, excessive "bleeding" can weaken trees.

When oaks or elms are wounded during a critical time of year (usually spring for oaks, or throughout the growing season for elms) — either from storms, other unforeseen mechanical wounds, or from necessary branch removals — some type of wound dressing should be applied to the wound. Do this immediately after the wound is created. In most other instances, wound dressings are unnecessary, and may even be detrimental. Wound dressings will not stop decay or cure infectious diseases. They may actually interfere with the protective benefits of tree gums and resins, and prevent wound surfaces from closing as quickly as they might under natural conditions. The only benefit of wound dressings is to prevent introduction of pathogens in the specific cases of Dutch elm disease and oak wilt.

PRUNING GUIDELINES

- To encourage the development of a strong, healthy tree, consider the following guidelines when pruning.
- *General* Prune first for safety, next for health, and finally for aesthetics.
- Never prune trees that are touching or near utility lines; instead consult your local utility company.
- Avoid pruning trees when you might increase susceptibility to important pests (e.g. in areas where oak wilt exists, avoid pruning oaks in the spring and early summer; prune trees susceptible to fireblight only during the dormant season).

Use the following decision guide for size of branches to be removed:

1. under 5 cm diameter - go ahead;
2. between 5 and 10 cm diameter - think twice; and
3. greater than 10 cm diameter - have a good reason.

Specialized Terms

Branch Axil: the angle formed where a branch joins another branch or stem of a woody plant.

Branch Bark Ridge: a ridge of bark that forms in a branch crotch and partially around the stem resulting from the growth of the stem and branch tissues against one another.

Branch Collar: a "shoulder" or bulge formed at the base of a branch by the annual production of overlapping layers of branch and stem tissues.

Crown Raising: a method of pruning to provide clearance for pedestrians, vehicles, buildings, lines of sight, and vistas by removing lower branches.

Crown Reduction Pruning: a method of pruning used to reduce the height of a tree. Branches are cut back to laterals that are at least one-third the diameter of the limb being removed.

Crown Thinning: a method of pruning to increase light penetration and air movement through the crown of a tree by selective removal of branches.

Callus: below.

Decurrent: a major tree form resulting from weak apical control. Trees with this form have several to many lateral branches that compete with the central stem for dominance resulting in a spherical or globose crown. Most hardwood trees have decurrent forms.

Epicormic Sprout: a shoot that arises from latent or adventitious buds; also known as water sprouts that occur on stems and branches and suckers that are produced from the base of trees. In older wood, epicormic shoots often result from severe defoliation or radical pruning.

Excurrent: a major tree form resulting from strong apical control. Trees with this form have a strong central stem and pyramidal shape. Lateral branches rarely compete for dominance. Most conifers and a few hardwoods, such as sweetgum and tuliptree, have excurrent forms.

Flush Cuts: pruning cuts that originate inside the branch bark ridge or the branch collar, causing unnecessary injury to stem tissues.

Included Bark: bark enclosed between branches with narrow angles of attachment, forming a wedge between the branches.

Pollarding: the annual removal of all of the previous year's growth, resulting in a flush of slender shoots and branches each spring.

Stub Cuts: pruning cuts made too far outside the branch bark ridge or branch collar, that leave branch tissue attached to the stem.

Tipping: a poor maintenance practice used to control the size of tree crowns; involves the cutting of branches at right angles leaving long stubs.

Topping: a poor maintenance practice often used to control the size of trees; involves the indiscriminate cutting of branches and stems at right angles leaving long stubs. Synonyms include rounding-over, heading-back, dehorning, capping and hat-racking. Topping is often improperly referred to as pollarding.

Topiary: the pruning and training of a plant into a desired geometric or animal shape.

Woundwood: lignified, differentiated tissues produced on woody plants as a response to wounding (also known as callus tissue).

CHAPTER 4

Tree Leaves and Photosynthesis

INTRODUCTION

Leaf colour comes from *pigments*. Pigments are natural substances produced by leaf cells. The three pigments that color leaves are:

- *chlorophyll* (green);
- *carotenoid* (yellow, orange, and brown); and
- *anthocyanins* (red).

Chlorophyll is the most important of the three. Without the chlorophyll in leaves, trees wouldn't be able to use sunlight to produce food.

Carotenoid create bright yellows and oranges in familiar fruits and vegetables. Corn, carrots, and bananas are just a few of the many plants colored by carotenoid.

Anthocyanins add the color red to plants, including cranberries, red apples, cherries, strawberries and others.

Chlorophyll and carotenoid are in leaf cells all the time during the growing season. But the chlorophyll covers the carotenoid — that's why summer leaves are green, not yellow or orange. Most anthocyanins are produced only in autumn, and only under certain conditions. Not all trees can make anthocyanins.

As the Earth makes its 365-day journey around the sun, some parts of the planet will get fewer hours of sunlight at certain times of the year. In those regions, the days become shorter and the nights grow longer. The temperature slowly drops. Autumn comes, and then winter.

Trees respond to the decreasing amount of sunlight by producing less and less chlorophyll. Eventually, a tree stops producing chlorophyll. When that happens, the carotenoid already in the leaves can finally show through. The leaves become a bright rainbow of glowing yellows, sparkling oranges and warm browns. What about red leaves? Read on.

Perhaps you've noticed that in some years, the red fall colors seem brighter and more spectacular than in other years. The *temperature* and *cloud cover* can make a big difference in a tree's red colors from year to year.

When a number of warm, sunny autumn days and cool but not freezing nights come one after the other, it's going to be a good year for reds. In the daytime, the leaves can produce lots of sugar, but the cool night temperatures prevent the sugar sap from flowing through the leaf veins and down into the branches and trunk. Anthocyanins to the rescue! Researchers have found out that anthocyanins are produced as a form of protection. They allow the plant to recover nutrients in the leaves before they fall off. This helps make sure that the tree will be ready for the next growing season. Anthocyanins give leaves the bright, brilliant shades of red, purple and crimson.

The yellow, gold and orange colors created by carotenoid remain fairly constant from year to year. That's because carotenoid are always present in leaves, and the amount does not change in response to weather.

The amount of rain in a year also affects autumn leaf color. A severe drought can delay the arrival of fall colors by a few weeks. A warm, wet period during fall will lower the intensity, or brightness, of autumn colors. A severe frost will kill the leaves, turning them brown and causing them to drop early. The best autumn colors come when there's been:

- a warm, wet spring;
- a summer that's not too hot or dry; and
- a fall with plenty of warm sunny days and cool nights.

You can use fall leaf color to help identify different tree species. Look for these leaf colors on the trees in your neighbourhood:

- Oaks: red, brown or russet
- Hickories: golden bronze
- Dogwood: purple-red
- Birch: bright yellow
- paper birch
- yellow birch
- Poplar: golden yellow
- Maple trees show a whole range of colours.
- Sugar Maple: orange-red
- Black Maple: glowing yellow
- Red Maple: bright scarlet

A tree's roots, branches and twigs can endure freezing temperatures, but most leaves are not so tough. On a *broadleaf* tree — say a maple or a birch — the tender thin leaves, made up of cells filled with water sap, will freeze in winter. Any plant tissue unable to live through the winter must be sealed off and shed to ensure the tree's survival.

As sunlight decreases in autumn, the veins that carry sap into and out of a leaf gradually close. A layer of cells, called the *separation layer*, forms at the base of the leaf stem. When this layer is complete, the leaf is separated from the tissue that connected it to the branch, and it falls. Oak leaves are the exception. The separation layer never fully detaches the dead oak leaves, and they remain on the tree through winter.

Evergreen Trees

Pines, spruces, cedars and firs — don't lose their leaves, or needles, in winter. The needles are covered with a heavy wax coating and the fluids inside the cells contain substances that resist freezing. Evergreen leaves can live for several years before they fall and are replaced by new growth.

On the ground, fallen leaves are broken down by bacteria, fungi, earthworms and other organisms. The decomposed leaves restock the soil with nutrients, and become part of the spongy humus layer on the forest floor that absorb and hold rainfall. In nature, nothing goes to waste!

PHOTOSYNTHESIS

The word comes from the Greek - *(photo-)*, "light," and *(synthesis)*, "placing with."

Photosynthesis is a metabolic pathway that converts light energy into chemical energy. Its initial substrates are carbon dioxide and water; the energy source is sunlight (electromagnetic radiation); and the end-products are oxygen and (energy-containing) carbohydrates, such as sucrose, glucose or starch. This process is one of the most important biochemical pathways, since nearly all life on Earth either directly or indirectly depends on it as a source of energy. It is a complex process occurring in plants, algae, as well as bacteria such as cyanobacteria. Photosynthetic organisms are also referred to as *photoautotrophs*.

Photosynthesis uses light energy and carbon dioxide to make triose phosphates (G3P). G3P is generally considered the first end-product of photosynthesis. It can be used as a source of metabolic energy, or combined and rearranged to form monosaccharide or disaccharide sugars, such as glucose or sucrose, respectively, which can be transported to other cells, stored as insoluble polysaccharides such as starch, or converted to structural carbohydrates, such as cellulose or glucans.

A commonly used slightly simplified equation for photosynthesis is:

$$6\,CO_{2(g)} + 12\,H_2O_{(l)} + \text{photons} \rightarrow C_6H_{12}O_{6(aq)} + 6\,O_{2(g)} + 6\,H_2O_{(l)}$$

carbon dioxide + water + light energy → glucose + oxygen + water

The equation is often presented in introductory chemistry texts in an even more simplified form as:

$$6\ CO_{2(g)} + 6\ H_2O_{(l)} + \text{photons} \rightarrow C_6H_{12}O_{6(aq)} + 6\ O_{2(g)}$$

Photosynthesis occurs in two stages. In the first stage, *light-dependent reactions* or *photosynthetic reactions* (also called the *Light Reactions*) capture the energy of light and use it to make high-energy molecules. During the second stage, the *light-independent reactions* (also called the Calvin-Benson Cycle, and formerly known as the *Dark Reactions*) use the high-energy molecules to capture and chemically reduce carbon dioxide (CO_2) (also called carbon fixation) to make the precursors of carbohydrates.

In the light reactions, one molecule of the pigment chlorophyll absorbs one photon and loses one electron. This electron is passed to a modified form of chlorophyll called pheophytin, which passes the electron to a quinone molecule, allowing the start of a flow of electrons down an electron transport chain that leads to the ultimate reduction of NADP to NADPH. In addition, this creates a proton gradient across the chloroplast membrane; its dissipation is used by ATP Synthase for the concomitant synthesis of ATP. The chlorophyll molecule regains the lost electron from a water molecule through a process called photolysis, which releases a dioxygen (O_2) molecule. In the Light-independent or dark reactions the enzyme RuBisCO captures CO_2 from the atmosphere and in a process that requires the newly formed NADPH, called the Calvin-Benson Cycle, releases three-carbon sugars, which are later combined to form sucrose and starch. Photosynthesis may simply be defined as the conversion of light energy into chemical energy by living organisms. It is affected by its surroundings, and the rate of photosynthesis is affected by the concentration of carbon dioxide in the air, the light intensity, and the temperature.

Photosynthesis uses only 1% of the entire electromagnetic spectrum, and 2% of the visible spectrum It has been estimated that the productivity of photosythesis is 115 petagrams (Pg, equals 10^{15} grams or 10^9 metric tons).

PHOTOAUTOTROPHS

Most plants are photoautotrophs, which means that they are able to synthesize food directly from inorganic compounds using light energy - for example from the sun, instead of eating other organisms or relying on nutrients derived from them. This is distinct from chemoautotrophs that do *not* depend on light energy, but use energy from inorganic compounds.

$$6\ CO_2 + 12\ H_2O \rightarrow C_6H_{12}O_6 + 6\ O_2 + 6\ H_2O$$

The energy for photosynthesis ultimately comes from absorbed photons and involves a reducing agent, which is water in the case of plants, releasing oxygen as product. The light energy is converted to chemical energy (known as light-dependent reactions), in the form of ATP and NADPH, which are used for synthetic reactions in photoautotrophs. The overall equation for the light-dependent reactions under the conditions of non-cyclic electron flow in green plants is:

$$2\ H_2O + 2\ NADP^+ + 2\ ADP + 2\ P_i + \text{light} \rightarrow 2\ NADPH + 2\ H^+ + 2\ ATP + O_2$$

Most notably, plants use the chemical energy to fix carbon dioxide into carbohydrates and other organic compounds through light-independent reactions. The overall equation for carbon fixation (sometimes referred to as carbon reduction) in green plants is

$$3\ CO_2 + 9\ ATP + 6\ NADPH + 6\ H^+ \rightarrow C_3H_6O_3\text{-phosphate} + 9\ ADP + 8\ P_i + 6\ NADP^+ + 3\ H_2O$$

To be more specific, carbon fixation produces an intermediate product, which is then converted to the final carbohydrate products. The carbon skeletons produced by photosynthesis are then variously used to form other organic compounds, such as the building material cellulose, as precursors for lipid and amino acid biosynthesis, or as a fuel in cellular respiration. The latter occurs not only in plants but also in animals when the energy from plants gets passed through a food chain. Organisms dependent on photosynthetic and chemosynthetic organisms are called heterotrophs. In general outline, cellular respiration is the opposite of photosynthesis: Glucose and other compounds are oxidized to produce carbon dioxide, water, and chemical energy. However, the two processes take place through a different sequence of chemical reactions and in different cellular compartments.

Plants absorb light primarily using the pigment chlorophyll, which is the reason that most plants have a green color. The function of chlorophyll is often supported by other accessory pigments such as carotenes and xanthophylls. Both chlorophyll and accessory pigments are contained in organelles (compartments within the cell) called chloroplasts. Although all cells in the green parts of a plant have chloroplasts, most of the energy is captured in the leaves. The cells in the interior tissues of a leaf, called the mesophyll, can contain between 450,000 and 800,000 chloroplasts for every square millimeter of leaf. The surface of the leaf is uniformly coated with a water-resistant waxy cuticle that protects the leaf from excessive evaporation of water and decreases the absorption of ultraviolet or blue light to reduce heating. The transparent epidermis layer allows light to pass through to the palisade mesophyll cells where most of the photosynthesis takes place.

Plants convert light into chemical energy with a maximum photosynthetic efficiency of approximately 6% By comparison solar panels convert light into electric energy at a photosynthetic efficiency of approximately 10-20%. Actual plant's photosynthetic efficiency varies with the frequency of the light being converted, light intensity, temperature and proportion of CO_2 in atmosphere.

In Algae and Bacteria

Algae come in multiple forms from multicellular organisms like kelp, to microscopic, single-cell organisms. Although they are not as complex as land plants, the biochemical process of photosynthesis is the same. Very much like plants, algae have chloroplasts and chlorophyll, but various accessory pigments are present in some algae such as phycocyanin, carotenes, and xanthophylls in green algae and phycoerythrin in red algae (rhodophytes), resulting in a wide variety of colors. Brown algae and diatoms contain fucoxanthol as their primary pigment. All algae produce oxygen, and many are autotrophic. However, some are heterotrophic, relying on materials produced by other organisms. For example, in coral reefs, there is a mutualistic relationship between zooxanthellae and the coral polyps.

Photosynthetic bacteria do not have chloroplasts (or any membrane-bound organelles). Instead, photosynthesis takes place directly within the cell. Cyanobacteria contain thylakoid membranes very similar to those in chloroplasts and are the only prokaryotes that perform oxygen-generating photosynthesis. In fact, chloroplasts are now considered to have evolved from an endosymbiotic bacterium, which was also an ancestor of cyanobacterium.

The other photosynthetic bacteria have a variety of different pigments, called bacteriochlorophylls, and use electron donors different from water and thus do not produce oxygen. Some bacteria, such as *Chromatium*, oxidize hydrogen sulfide instead of water for photosynthesis, producing sulfur as waste. Other photosynthetic bacteria oxidize ferrous iron to ferric iron, others nitrite to nitrate and still others use arsenites, producing arsenates.

All photosynthesizing organisms must be in the photic (light-receiving) zone, except for those near hydrothermal vents which give faint light.

PLANT CELLS WITH VISIBLE CHLOROPLASTS

Early photosynthetic systems, such as those from green and purple sulfur and green and purple non-sulfur bacteria, are thought to have been anoxygenic, using various molecules as electron donors. Green and purple sulfur bacteria are thought to have used hydrogen and sulfur as an electron donor. Green nonsulfur bacteria used various amino and other organic acids. Purple nonsulfur bacteria used a variety of non-specific organic molecules. The use of these molecules is consistent with the geological evidence that the atmosphere was highly reduced at that time. Fossils of what are thought to be filamentous photosynthetic organisms have been dated at 3.4 billion years old.

The main source of oxygen in the atmosphere is oxygenic photosynthesis, and its first appearance is sometimes referred to as the oxygen catastrophe. Geological evidence suggests that oxygenic photosynthesis, such as that in cyanobacteria, became important during the Paleoproterozoic era around 2 billion years ago. Modern photosynthesis in plants and most photosynthetic prokaryotes is oxygenic. Oxygenic photosynthesis uses water as an electron donor which is oxidized to molecular dioxygen (O_2) in the photosynthetic reaction center.

Origin of Chloroplasts

In plants photosynthesis occurs in organelles called chloroplasts. Chloroplasts have many similarities with photosynthetic bacteria including a circular chromosome, prokaryotic-type ribosomes, and similar proteins in the photosynthetic reaction center.

The endosymbiotic theory suggests that photosynthetic bacteria were acquired (by endocytosis) by early eukaryotic cells to form the first plant cells. Therefore, chloroplasts may be photosynthetic bacteria that adapted to life inside plant cells. Like mitochondria, chloroplasts still possess their own DNA, separate from the nuclear DNA of their plant host cells and the genes in this chloroplast DNA resemble those in cyanobacteria.

Marine molluscs *Elysia viridis* and *Elysia chlorotica* likewise maintain a symbiotic relationship with chloroplasts that they capture from the algae that they ingest. This allows the molluscs to survive solely by photosynthesis for several months at a time.

Cyanobacteria and the Evolution of Photosynthesis

The biochemical capacity to use water as the source for electrons in photosynthesis evolved once, in a common ancestor of extant cyanobacteria. The geological record indicates that this transforming event took place early in Earth's history, at least 2450-2320 million years ago (Ma), and possibly much earlier. Available evidence from geobiological studies of Archean (>2500 Ma) sedimentary rocks indicates that life existed 3500 Ma, but the question of when oxygenic photosynthesis evolved is still unanswered. A clear paleontological window on cyanobacterial evolution opened about 2000 Ma, revealing an already-diverse biota of blue-greens. Cyanobacteria remained principal primary producers throughout the Proterozoic Eon (2500-543 Ma), in part because the redox structure of the oceans favored photoautotrophs capable of nitrogen fixation. Green algae joined blue-greens as major primary producers on continental shelves near the end of the Proterozoic, but only with the Mesozoic (251-65 Ma) radiations of dinoflagellates, coccolithophorids, and diatoms did primary production in marine shelf waters take modern form. Cyanobacteria remain critical to marine ecosystems as primary producers in oceanic gyres, as agents of biological nitrogen fixation, and, in modified form, as the plastids of marine algae.

Light-dependent Reactions of Photosynthesis at the Thylakoid Membrane

The overall process of photosynthesis takes place in four stages. The first, energy transfer in antenna chlorophyll takes place in the femtosecond [1 femtosecond (fs) = $10,^{-15}$ s] to picosecond [1 picosecond (ps) = 10^{-12} s] time scale. The next phase, the transfer of electrons in photochemical reactions, takes place in the picosecond to nanosecond time scale [1 nanosecond (ns) = 10^{-9} s]. The third phase, the electron transport chain and ATP synthesis, takes place on the microsecond [1 microsecond (μs) = 10^{-6} s] to millisecond [1 millisecond (ms) = 10^{-3} s) time scale. The final phase is carbon fixation and export of stable products and takes place in the millisecond to second time scale. The first three stages occur in the thylakoid membranes.

LIGHT TO CHEMICAL ENERGY

The light energy is converted to chemical energy using the light-dependent reactions. This chemical energy production is about 5-6% efficient, with the majority of the light that strikes a plant reflected and not absorbed. However, of the energy that is absorbed, approximately 30-50% is captured as chemical energy. The products of the light-dependent reactions are ATP from photophosphorylation and NADPH from photoreduction. Both are then utilized as an energy source for the light-independent reactions.

Not all wavelengths of light can support photosynthesis. The photosynthetic action spectrum depends on the type of accessory pigments present. For example, in green plants, the action spectrum resembles the absorption spectrum for chlorophylls and carotenoids with peaks for violet-blue and red light. In red algae, the action spectrum overlaps with the absorption spectrum of phycobilins for blue-green light, which allows these algae to grow in deeper waters that filter out the longer wavelengths used by green plants. The non-absorbed part of the light spectrum is what gives photosynthetic organisms their color (e.g., green plants, red algae, purple bacteria) and is the least effective for photosynthesis in the respective organisms.

In plants, light-dependent reactions occur in the thylakoid membranes of the chloroplasts and use light energy to synthesize ATP and NADPH. The light-dependent reaction has two forms; cyclic and non-cyclic reaction. In the non-cyclic reaction, the photons are captured in the light-harvesting antenna complexes of photosystem II by chlorophyll and other accessory pigments (see diagram at right). When a chlorophyll molecule at the core of the photosystem II reaction center obtains sufficient excitation energy from the adjacent antenna pigments, an electron is transferred to the primary electron-acceptor molecule, Pheophytin, through a process called Photoinduced charge separation. These electrons are shuttled through an electron transport chain, the so called *Z-scheme* shown in the diagram, that initially functions to generate a chemiosmotic potential across the membrane. An ATP synthase enzyme uses the chemiosmotic potential to make ATP during photophosphorylation, whereas NADPH is a product of the terminal redox reaction in the *Z-scheme*. The electron enters the Photosystem I molecule. The electron is excited due to the light absorbed by the photosystem. A second electron carrier accepts the electron, which again is passed down lowering energies of electron acceptors. The energy created by the electron acceptors is used to move hydrogen ions across the thylakoid membrane into the lumen. The electron is used to reduce the co-enzyme NADP, which has functions in the light-independent reaction. The cyclic reaction is similar to that of the non-cyclic, but differs in the form that it generates only ATP, and no reduced NADP (NADPH) is created. The cyclic reaction takes place only at photosystem I. Once the electron is displaced from the photosystem, the electron is passed down the electron acceptor molecules and returns back to photosystem I, from where it was emitted, hence the name *cyclic reaction*.

Water Photolysis

The NADPH is the main reducing agent in chloroplasts, providing a source of energetic electrons to other reactions. Its production leaves chlorophyll with a deficit of electrons (oxidized), which must be obtained from some other reducing agent. The excited electrons lost from chlorophyll in photosystem I are replaced from the electron transport chain by plastocyanin. However, since photosystem II includes the first steps of the *Z-scheme*, an external source of electrons is required to reduce its oxidized *chlorophyll a* molecules. The source of electrons in green-plant and cyanobacterial photosynthesis is water. Two water molecules are oxidized by four successive charge-separation reactions by photosystem II to yield a molecule of diatomic oxygen and four hydrogen ions; the electron yielded in each step is transferred to a redox-active tyrosine residue that then reduces the photoxidized paired-chlorophyll *a* species called P680 that serves as the primary (light-driven) electron donor in the photosystem II reaction center. The oxidation of water is catalyzed in photosystem II by a redox-active structure that contains four manganese ions and a calcium ion; this oxygen-evolving complex binds two water molecules and stores the four oxidizing equivalents that are required to drive the water-oxidizing reaction. Photosystem II is the only known biological enzyme that carries out this oxidation of water. The hydrogen ions contribute to the transmembrane chemiosmotic potential that leads to ATP synthesis. Oxygen is a waste product of light-independent reactions, but the majority of organisms on Earth use oxygen for cellular respiration, including photosynthetic organisms.

Quantum Mechanical Effects

Through photosynthesis, sunlight energy is transferred to molecular reaction centers for conversion into chemical energy with nearly 100-percent efficiency. The transfer of the solar energy takes place almost instantaneously, so little energy is wasted as heat. Of the total incident solar radiation only 43% can be used (only light in the range 400-700 nm), 80% of light makes it through the canopy, photosynthesis stores 28.6% of the energy, and plant respiration uses some energy which leaves 67% of the stored energy behind. This brings the actual efficiency of photosynthesis to about 6.6%.

A study led by researchers with the U.S. Department of Energy's Lawrence Berkeley National Laboratory (Berkeley Lab) and the University of California at Berkeley suggests that long-lived wavelike electronic quantum coherence plays an important part in this instantaneous transfer of energy by allowing the photosynthetic system to simultaneously try each potential energy pathway and choose the most efficient option. Results of the study are presented in the April 12, 2007 issue of the journal *Nature*.

GEN AND PHOTOSYNTHESIS

With respect to oxygen and photosynthesis, there are two important concepts.

- Plant and cyanobacterial (blue-green algae) cells *also use oxygen* for cellular respiration, although they have a net output of oxygen since much more is produced during photosynthesis.
- Oxygen is a *product of the light-driven water-oxidation reaction catalyzed by photosystem II*; it is not generated by the fixation of carbon dioxide. Consequently, the source of oxygen during photosynthesis is water, not carbon dioxide.

Bacterial Variation

The concept that oxygen production is not directly associated with the fixation of carbon dioxide was first proposed by Cornelis Van Niel in the 1930s, who studied photosynthetic bacteria. Aside from the cyanobacteria, bacteria only have one photosystem and use reducing agents other than water. They get electrons from a variety of different inorganic chemicals including sulfide or hydrogen, so for most of these bacteria oxygen is not produced.

Others, such as the halophiles (an Archaea), produced so-called purple membranes where the bacteriorhodopsin could harvest light and produce energy. The purple membranes was one of the first to be used to demonstrate the chemiosmotic theory: light hit the membranes and the pH of the solution that contained the purple membranes dropped as protons were pumping out of the membrane.

The fixation or reduction of carbon dioxide is a light-independent process in which carbon dioxide combines with a five-carbon sugar, ribulose 1,5-bisphosphate (RuBP), to yield two molecules of a three-carbon compound, glycerate 3-phosphate (GP), also known as 3-phosphoglycerate (PGA). GP, in the presence of ATP and NADPH from the light-dependent stages, is reduced to glyceraldehyde 3-phosphate (G3P). This product is also referred to as 3-phosphoglyceraldehyde (PGAL) or even as triose phosphate. Triose is a 3-carbon sugar (see carbohydrates). Most (5 out of 6 molecules) of the G3P produced is used to regenerate RuBP so the process can continue (see Calvin-Benson cycle). The 1 out of 6 molecules of the triose phosphates not "recycled" often condense to form hexose phosphates, which ultimately yield sucrose, starch and cellulose. The sugars produced during carbon metabolism yield carbon skeletons that can be used for other metabolic reactions like the production of amino acids and lipids.

C_4 AND C_3 PHOTOSYNTHESIS AND CAM

In hot and dry conditions, plants will close their stomata to prevent loss of water. Under these conditions, CO_2 will decrease, and dioxygen gas, produced by the light reactions of photosynthesis, will increase in the leaves, causing an increase of photorespiration by the oxygenase activity of ribulose-1,5-bisphosphate carboxylase/oxygenase and decrease in carbon fixation. Some plants have evolved mechanisms to increase the CO_2 concentration in the leaves under these conditions.

C4 plants chemically fix carbon dioxide in the cells of the mesophyll by adding it to the three-carbon molecule phosphoenolpyruvate (PEP), a reaction catalyzed by an enzyme called PEP carboxylase and which creates the four-carbon organic acid, oxaloacetic acid. Oxaloacetic acid or malate synthesized by this process is then translocated to specialized bundle sheath cells where the enzyme, rubisco, and other Calvin cyle enzymes are located, and where CO_2 released by decarboxylation of the four-carbon acids is then fixed by rubisco activity to the three-carbon sugar 3-phosphoglycerate. The physical separation of rubisco from the oxygen-generating light reactions reduces photorespiration and increases CO_2 fixation and thus photosynthetic capacity of the leaf. C_4 plants can produce more sugar than C_3 plants in conditions of high light and temperature. Many important crop plants are C_4 plants including maize, sorghum, sugarcane, and millet. Plants lacking PEP-carboxylase are called *C_3 plants* because the primary carboxylation reaction, catalyzed by Rubiso, produces the three-carbon sugar 3-phosphoglycerate directly in the Calvin-Benson Cycle.

Xerophytes such as cacti and most succulents also use PEP carboxylase to capture carbon dioxide in a process called Crassulacean acid metabolism (CAM). In contrast to C_4 metabolism, which *physically* separates the CO_2 fixation to PEP from the Calvin cycle, CAM only *temporally* separates these two processes. CAM plants have a different leaf anatomy than C_4 plants, and fix the CO_2 at night, when their stomata are open. CAM plants store the CO_2 mostly in the form of malic acid via carboxylation of phosphoenolpyruvate to oxaloacetate, which is then reduced to malate. Decarboxylation of malate during the day releases CO_2 inside the leaves thus allowing carbon fixation to 3-phosphoglycerate by rubisco.

Although some of the steps in photosynthesis are still not completely understood, the overall photosynthetic equation has been known since the 1800s.

Jan van Helmont began the research of the process in the mid-1600s when he carefully measured the mass of the soil used by a plant and the mass of the plant as it grew. After noticing that the soil mass changed very little, he hypothesized that the mass of the growing plant must come from the water, the only substance he added to the potted plant. His hypothesis was partially accurate - much of the gained mass also comes from carbon dioxide as well as water. However, this was a signaling point to the idea that the bulk of a plant's biomass comes from the inputs of photosynthesis, not the soil itself.

Joseph Priestley, a chemist and minister, discovered that when he isolated a volume of air under an inverted jar, and burned a candle in it, the candle would burn out very quickly, much before it ran out of wax. He further discovered that a mouse could similarly "injure" air. He then showed that the air that had been "injured" by the candle and the mouse could be restored by a plant.

In 1778, Jan Ingenhousz, court physician to the Austrian Empress, repeated Priestley's experiments. He discovered that it was the influence of sunlight on the plant that could cause it to rescue a mouse in a matter of hours.

In 1796, Jean Senebier, a Swiss pastor, botanist, and naturalist, demonstrated that green plants consume carbon dioxide and release oxygen under the influence of light. Soon afterwards, Nicolas-Théodore de Saussure showed that the increase in mass of the plant as it grows could not be due only to uptake of CO_2, but also to the incorporation of water. Thus the basic reaction by which photosynthesis is used to produce food (such as glucose) was outlined.

Cornelis Van Niel made key discoveries explaining the chemistry of photosynthesis. By studying purple sulfur bacteria and green bacteria he was the first scientist to demonstrate that photosynthesis is a light-dependent redox reaction, in which hydrogen reduces carbon dioxide.

Robert Emerson discovered two light reactions by testing plant productivity using different wavelengths of light. With the red alone, the light reactions were suppressed. When blue and red were combined, the output was much more substantial. Thus, there were two photosystems, one aborbing up to 600 nm wavelengths, the other up to 700. The former is known as PSII, the latter is PSI. PSI contains only chlorophyll a, PSII contains primarily chlorophyll a with most of the available chlorophyll b, among other pigments.

Further experiments to prove that the oxygen developed during the photosynthesis of green plants came from water, were performed by Robert Hill in 1937 and 1939. He showed that isolated chloroplasts give off oxygen in the presence of unnatural reducing agents like iron oxalate, ferricyanide or benzoquinone after exposure to light. The Hill reaction is as follows:

$$2\ H_2O + 2\ A + (\text{light, chloroplasts}) \rightarrow 2\ AH_2 + O_2$$

where A is the electron acceptor. Therefore, in light the electron acceptor is reduced and oxygen is evolved. Cyt b_6, now known as a plastoquinone, is one electron acceptor.

Samuel Ruben and Martin Kamen used radioactive isotopes to determine that the oxygen liberated in photosynthesis came from the water.

Melvin Calvin and Andrew Benson, along with James Bassham, elucidated the path of carbon assimilation (the photosynthetic carbon reduction cycle) in plants. The carbon reduction cycle is known as the Calvin cycle, which inappropriately ignores the contribution of Bassham and Benson. Many scientists refer to the cycle as the Calvin-Benson Cycle, Benson-Calvin, and some even call it the Calvin-Benson-Bassham (or CBB) Cycle.

A Nobel Prize winning scientist, Rudolph A. Marcus, was able to discover the function and significance of the electron transport chain.

There are three main factors affecting photosynthesis and several corollary factors. The three main are:

- Light irradiance and wavelength;
- Carbon dioxide concentration
- Temperature.

Light Intensity (Irradiance), Wavelength and Temperature

In the early 1900s Frederick Frost Blackman along with Gabrielle Matthaei investigated the effects of light intensity (irradiance) and temperature on the rate of carbon assimilation.

- At constant temperature, the rate of carbon assimilation varies with irradiance, initially increasing as the irradiance increases. However at higher irradiance this relationship no longer holds and the rate of carbon assimilation reaches a plateau.
- At constant irradiance, the rate of carbon assimilation increases as the temperature is increased over a limited range. This effect is only seen at high irradiance levels. At low irradiance, increasing the temperature has little influence on the rate of carbon assimilation.

These two experiments illustrate vital points: firstly, from research it is known that photochemical reactions are not generally affected by temperature. However, these experiments clearly show that temperature affects the rate of carbon assimilation, so there must be two sets of reactions in the full process of carbon assimilation. These are of course the light-dependent 'photochemical' stage and the light-independent, temperature-dependent stage. Second, Blackman's experiments illustrate the concept of limiting factors. Another limiting factor is the wavelength of light. Cyanobacteria, which reside several meters underwater, cannot receive the correct wavelengths required to cause photoinduced charge separation in conventional photosynthetic pigments. To combat this problem, a series of proteins with different pigments surround the reaction center. This unit is called a phycobilisome.

Carbon Dioxide Levels and Photorespiration

As carbon dioxide concentrations rise, the rate at which sugars are made by the light-independent reactions increases until limited by other factors. RuBisCO, the enzyme that captures carbon dioxide in the light-independent reactions, has a binding affinity for both carbon dioxide and oxygen. When the concentration of carbon dioxide is high, RuBisCO will fix carbon dioxide. However, if the oxygen concentration is high, RuBisCO will bind oxygen instead of carbon dioxide. This process, called photorespiration, uses energy, but does not make temperature.

RuBisCO oxygenase activity is disadvantageous to plants for several reasons:

- One product of oxygenase activity is phosphoglycolate (2 carbon) instead of 3-phosphoglycerate (3 carbon). Phosphoglycolate cannot be metabolized by the Calvin-Benson cycle and represents carbon lost from the cycle. A high oxygenase activity, therefore, drains the sugars that are required to recycle ribulose 5-bisphosphate and for the continuation of the Calvin-Benson cycle.
- Phosphoglycolate is quickly metabolized to glycolate that is toxic to a plant at a high concentration; it inhibits photosynthesis.
- Salvaging glycolate is an energetically expensive process that uses the glycolate pathway and only 75% of the carbon is returned to the Calvin-Benson cycle as 3-phosphoglycerate.

  A highly-simplified summary is:

- 2 glycolate + ATP ? 3-phophoglycerate + carbon dioxide + ADP + NH_3

The salvaging pathway for the products of RuBisCO oxygenase activity is more commonly known as photorespiration, since it is characterized by light-dependent oxygen consumption and the release of carbon dioxide.

CHAPTER 5

Tree Stem

INTRODUCTION

A stem is one of two main structural axes of a vascular plant. The stem is normally divided into nodes and internodes, the nodes hold buds which grow into one or more leaves, inflorescence (flowers), cones or other stems etc. The internodes act as spaces that distance one node from another. The term shoots is often confused with stems; shoots generally refer to new fresh plant growth and does include stems but also to other structures like leaves or flowers. The other main structural axis of plants is the root. In most plants stems are located above the soil surface but some plants have underground stems.

Stems have four main functions which are:

- Support for and the elevation of leaves, flowers and fruits. The stems keep the leaves in the light and provide a place for the plant to keep its flowers and fruits.
- Transport of fluids between the roots and the shoots in the xylem and phloem.
- Storage of nutrients.
- The production of new living tissue. The normal life span of plant cells is one to three years. Stems have cells called meristems that annually generate new living tissue.

Specialized Terms for Stems

Stems are often specialized for storage, asexual reproduction, protection or photosynthesis, including the following:

- *Acaulescent* - plants with very short stems that appear to have no stems. The leaves appear to rise out of the ground, e.g. some Viola.
- *Arborescent* - tree like with woody stems normally with a single trunk.
- *Bud* - an embryonic shoot with immature stem tip.
- *Bulb* - a short vertical underground stem with fleshy storage leaves attached, e.g. onion, daffodil, tulip. Bulbs often function in reproduction by splitting to form new bulbs or producing small new bulbs termed bulblets. Bulbs are a combination of stem and leaves so may better be considered as leaves because the leaves make up the greater part.
- *Caespitose* - when stems grow in a tangled mass or clump or in low growing mats.
- *Cladophyll* - a flattened stem that appears leaf like and is specialized for photosynthesis, e.g. asparagus, cactus pads.
- *Climbing* - stems that cling or wrap around other plants or structures.
- *Corm* - a short enlarged underground, storage stem, e.g. taro, crocus, gladiolus.
- *Decumbent* - stems that lay flat on the ground and turn upwards at the ends.
- *Fruticose* - stems that grow shrub like with woody like habit.
- Herbaceous - non woody, they die at the end of the growing season.
- *Pseudostem* - A false stem made of the rolled bases of leaves, which may be 2 or 3 m tall as in banana.
- *Rhizome* - a horizontal underground stem that functions mainly in reproduction but also in storage, e.g. most ferns, iris.

- *Runner (plant part)* - a type of stolon, horizontally growing on top of the ground and rooting at the nodes. e.g. strawberry, spider plant.
- *Scape* - a stem that holds flowers that comes out of the ground and has no normal leaves. Hosta, Lily, Iris.
- *Stolons* - a horizontal stem that produces rooted plantlets at its nodes and ends, forming near the surface of the ground.
- *Tree* - a woody stem that is longer than 5 meters with a main trunk.
- *Thorns* - a reduced stem with a sharp point and rounded shape. e.g. honey locust, hawthorn.
- *Tuber* - a swollen, underground storage stem adapted for storage and reproduction, e.g. potato.
- *Woody* - hard textured stems with secondary xylem.

STEM STRUCTURE

Stem usually consist of three tissues, dermal tissue, ground tissue and vascular tissue. The dermal tissue covers the outer surface of the stem and usually functions to waterproof, protect and control gas exchange. The ground tissue usually consists mainly of parenchyma cells and fills in around the vascular tissue. It sometimes functions in photosynthesis. Vascular tissue provides long distance transport and structural support. Most or all ground tissue may be lost in woody stems. The dermal tissue of aquatic plants stems may lack the waterproofing found in aerial stems. The arrangement of the vascular tissues varies widely among plant species.

DICOT STEMS

Dicot stems with primary growth have pith in the centre, with vascular bundles forming a distinct ring visible when the stem is viewed in cross section. The outside of the stem is covered with an epidermis, which is covered by a waterproof cuticle. The epidermis also may contain stomata for gas exchange and hairs. A cortex of parenchyma cells lies between the epidermis and vascular bundles.

Woody dicots and many nonwoody dicots have secondary growth originating from their lateral or secondary meristems: the vascular cambium and the cork cambium or phellogen. The vascular cambium forms between the xylem and phloem in the vascular bundles and connects to form a continuous cylinder. The vascular cambium cells divide to produce secondary xylem to the inside and secondary phloem to the outside. As the stem increases in diameter due to production of secondary xylem and secondary phloem, the cortex and epidermis are eventually destroyed. Before the cortex is destroyed, a cork cambium develops there. The cork cambium divides to produce waterproof cork cells externally and sometimes phelloderm cells internally. Those three tissues form the periderm, which replaces the epidermis in function. Areas of loosely-packed cells in the periderm that function in gas exchange are called lenticels.

Secondary xylem is commercially important as wood. The seasonal variation in growth from the vascular cambium is what creates yearly tree rings in temperate climates. Tree rings are the basis of dendrochronology, which dates wooden objects and associated artifacts. Dendroclimatology is the use of tree rings as a record of past climates. The aerial stem of an adult tree is called a trunk. The dead, usually darker inner wood of a large diameter trunk is termed the heartwood. The outer, living wood is termed the sapwood.

Monocot Stems

Vascular bundles are present throughout the monocot stem, although concentrated towards the outside. This differs from the dicot stem that has a ring of vascular bundles and often none in the center. The shoot apex in monocot stems is more elongated. Leaf sheathes grow up around it, protecting it. This is true to some extent of almost all monocots. Monocots rarely produce secondary growth and are therefore seldom woody. However, many monocot stems increase in diameter via anamolous secondary growth.

Gymnosperm Stems

All gymnosperms are woody plants. Their stems are similar in structure to woody dicots except that most gymnosperms produce only tracheids in their xylem, not the vessels found in dicots. Gymnosperm wood also often contains resin ducts. Woody dicots are called hardwoods, e.g. oak, maple and walnut. In contrast, softwoods are gymnosperms, such as pine, spruce and fir.

Fern Stems

Most ferns have rhizomes with no vertical stem. The exception is tree ferns, with vertical stems up to about 20 meters. The stem anatomy of ferns is more complicated than that of dicots because fern stems often have one or more leaf gaps in cross section. A leaf gap is where the vascular tissue branches off to a frond. In cross section, the vascular tissue does not form a complete cylinder where a leaf gap occurs. Fern stems may have solenosteles or dictyosteles or variations of them. Many fern stems have phloem tissue on both sides of the xylem in cross-section.

ECONOMIC IMPORTANCE

There are thousands of species whose stems have economic uses. Stems provide a few major staple crops such as potato and taro. Sugar cane stems are a major source of sugar. Maple sugar is obtained from trunks of maple trees. Vegetables from stems are asparagus, bamboo shoots, cactus pads or nopalitos, kohlrabi, and water chestnut. The spice, cinnamon is bark from a tree trunk. Cellulose from tree trunks is a food additive in bread, grated Parmesan cheese, and other processed foods. Gum arabic is an important food additive obtained from the trunks of *Acacia senegal* trees. Chicle, the main ingredient in chewing gum, is obtained from trunks of the chicle tree.

Medicines obtained from stems include quinine from the bark of cinchona trees, camphor distilled from wood of a tree in the same genus that provides cinnamon, and the muscle relaxant curare from the bark of tropical vines.

Wood is a used in thousands of ways, e.g. buildings, furniture, boats, airplanes, wagons, car parts, musical instruments, sports equipment, railroad ties, utility poles, fence posts, pilings, toothpicks, matches, plywood, coffins, shingles, barrel staves, toys, tool handles, picture frames, veneer, charcoal and firewood. Wood pulp is widely used to make paper, cardboard, cellulose sponges, cellophane and some important plastics and textiles, such as cellulose acetate and rayon. Bamboo stems also have hundreds of uses, including paper, buildings, furniture, boats, musical instruments, fishing poles, water pipes, plant stakes, and scaffolding. Trunks of palm trees and tree ferns are often used for building. Reed stems are also important building materials in some areas.

Tannins used for tanning leather are obtained from the wood of certain trees, such as quebracho. Cork is obtained from the bark of the cork oak. Rubber is obtained from the trunks of *Hevea brasiliensis*. Rattan, used for furniture and baskets, is made from the stems of tropical vining palms. Bast fibers for textiles and rope are obtained from stems include flax, hemp, jute and ramie. The earliest paper was obtained from the stems of papyrus by the ancient Egyptians.

Amber is fossilized sap from tree trunks; it is used for jewelry and may contain ancient animals. Resins from conifer wood are used to produce turpentine and rosin. Tree bark is often used as a mulch and in growing media for container plants.

Some ornamental plants are grown mainly for their attractive stems, e.g.:

- White bark of paper birch
- Twisted branches of corkscrew willow and Harry Lauder's walking stick (*Corylus avellana* 'Contorta')
- Red, peeling bark of paperbark maple

EPIDERMIS

The epidermis is the outer single-layered group of cells covering a plant, especially the leaf and young tissues of a vascular plant including stems and roots. Epidermis and periderm are the dermal tissues in vascular plants. The epidermis forms the boundary between the plant and the external world. The epidermis serves several functions: protection against water loss, regulation of gas exchange, secretion of metabolic compounds, and (especially in roots) absorption of water and mineral nutrients. The epidermis of most leaves shows dorsoventral anatomy: the upper (adaxial) and lower (abaxial) surfaces have somewhat different construction and may serve different functions.

The epidermis is the outermost cell layer of the primary plant body, it is the dermal tissue system of leaves, stems, roots, flowers, fruits, and seeds, it is usually transparent (epidermal cells lack chloroplasts, except for the guard cells.) The cells of the epidermis are structurally and functionally variable. Most plants have an epidermis that is only one cell layer thick, but some plants like *Ficus elastica* and *Peperomia*, have periclinal division within the protoderm with in the leaves causing a multiple layered epidermis. Epidermal cells are tightly linked to each other and provide mechanical protection to the plant. The walls of the epidermal cells of the above ground parts of plants contain cutin and are covered with a cuticle that reduces water loss. The cuticle is sometimes covered with wax in smooth sheets or long filaments, this wax causes the whitish or bluish color of some leaves. The cuticle may be thinner on the lower leaf epidermis than on the upper epidermis; and is thicker on leaves from dry climates as compared with those from wet climates.

The epidermal tissue includes several differentiated cell types: epidermal cells, guard cells, subsidiary cells, and epidermal hairs (trichomes). The epidermal cells are the most numerous, largest, and least specialized. These are typically more elongated in the leaves of monocots than in those of dicots.

Trichomes or hairs grow out from the epidermis in many species. In root epidermis, epidermal hairs, termed root hairs are common and are specialized for absorption of water and mineral nutrients. In plants with secondary growth, the epidermis of roots and stems is usually replaced by a periderm through the action of a cork cambium.

GUARD CELLS

The leaf and stem epidermis is covered with pores called stomata (sing., stoma), part of a stoma complex consisting of a pore surrounded on each side by chloroplast-containing guard cells, and two to four subsidiary cells that lack chloroplasts. The stoma complex regulates the exchange of gases and water vapor between the outside air and the interior of the leaf. Typically, the stomata are more numerous over the abaxial (lower) epidermis of the leaf than the (adaxial) upper epidermis. An exception is floating leaves where most or all stomata are on the upper surface. Vertical leaves, such as those of many grasses, often have roughly equal numbers of stomata on both surfaces. The number of stomata varies from about 1,000 to over 100,000 per square centimeter of leaf surface.

The stoma is bounded by two guard cells. The guard cells differ from the epidermal cells in the following aspects:

- The guard cells are bean-shaped in surface view, while the epidermal cells are irregular in shape;
- The guard cells contain chloroplasts, so they can manufacture food by photosynthesis (The epidermal cells do not contain chloroplasts);
- Guard Cells are the only epidermal cells that can make sugar. According to one theory, in sunlight the concentration of potassium ions (K+) increases in the guard cells. This, together with the sugars formed, lowers the water potential in the guard cells. As a result, water from other cells enter the guard cells by osmosis so they swell and become turgid. Because the guard cells have a thicker cellulose wall on one side of the cell, i.e. the side around the stomatal pore, the swollen guard cells become curved and pull the stomata open.

At night, the sugar is used up and water leaves the guard cells, so they become flaccid and the stomatal pore closes. In this way, they reduce the amount of water vapour escaping from the leaf.

Scanning electron microscope image of *Nicotiana alata* leaf's epidermis, showing trichomes (hair-like appendages) and stomata (eye-shaped slits, visible at full resolution)

The plant epidermis consists of three main cell types: pavement cells, guard cells and their subsidiary cells that surround the stomata and trichomes, otherwise known as leaf hairs. The epidermis of petals also form a variation of trichomes called conical cells. These cells all develop from the pavement cells, which make up the majority of the plants surface cells. In short, cellular differentiation of the epidermal cells is controlled by two major factors: genetics and environmental conditions.

Trichomes develop at a distinct phase during the actual leaf development, under the control of two major trichome specification genes: *TTG* and *GL1*. The process may be controlled by the plant hormones gibberellins, and even if not completely controlled, gibberellins certainly have an effect on the development of the leaf hairs. *GL1* causes endoreplication, the replication of DNA without subsequent cell division as well as cell expansion. *GL1* turns on the expression of a second gene for trichome formation, *GL2*, which controls the final stages of trichome formation causing the cellular outgrowth.

Arabidopsis uses the products of inhibitory genes to control the patterning of trichomes, such as *TTG* and *TRY*. The products of these genes will diffuse into the lateral cells, preventing them from forming trichomes and in the case of *TRY* promoting the formation of pavement cells.

As previously mentioned, conical cells are a form of trichome that occurs on the petals of flowers. Expression of the gene *MIXTA*, or its analogue in other species, later in the process of cellular differentiation will cause the formation of conical cells over trichomes. *MIXTA* is a transcription factor.

Stomatal pattering is a much more controlled process, as the stoma effect the plants water retention and respiration capabilities. As a consequence of these important functions, differentiation of cells to form stomata is also subject to environmental conditions to a much greater degree then other epidermal cell types.

Stomata are holes in the plant epidermis that are surrounded by two guard cells, which control the opening and closing of the aperture. These guard cells are in turn surrounded by subsidiary cells which provide a supporting role for the guard cells.

Stomata begin as stomatal meristemoids. The process varies between dicots and monocots. Spacing is thought to be essentially random in dicots though mutants do show it is under some form of genetic control, but it is more controlled in monocots, where stomata arise from specific asymmetric divisions of protodermal cells. The smaller of the two cells produced becomes the guard mother cells. Adjacent epidermal cells will also divide asymmetrically to form the subsidiary cells.

Because stomata play such an important role in the plants survival, collecting information of there differentiation if difficult by the traditional means of genetic manipulation, as stomatal mutants tend to be unable to survive. Thus the control of the process is not well understood. Some genes have been identified. *TMM* is thought to control the timing of stomatal initiation specification and *FLP* is thought to be involved in preventing further division of the guard cells once they are formed.

Environmental conditions affect the development of stomata, in particular their density on the leaf surface. It is thought that plant hormones, such as ethylene and cytokines, control the stomata's developmental response to the environmental conditions. Accumulation of these hormones appears to cause increased stomatal density such as when the plants are kept in closed environments.

Stomatal cells only occur on the leaf epidermis, and it is thought that inhibitory signals must occur on other parts of the plants epidermis to prevent stomatal formation there. These signals could be hormonal, or perhaps gene products transmitted from underlying tissues via the plasmodesmata.

GROUND TISSUE

The types of ground tissue found in plants develop from *ground tissue* meristem and consists of three simple tissues:

- Parenchyma (cells with thin primary walls that retain their protoplasm);
- Collenchyma (cells with thick primary walls that retain their protoplasm);
- Sclerenchyma (cells with lignified secondary walls that have lost their protoplasm at maturity, i.e. are 'dead').

Parenchyma

Parenchyma is the most common and versatile ground tissue. It forms, for example, the cortex and pith of stems, the cortex of roots, the mesophyll of leaves, the pulp of fruits, and the endosperm of seeds. Parenchyma cells are living cells and may remain meristematic at maturity, meaning that they are capable of cell division. They have thin but flexible cellulose cell walls, and are generally polygonal when close-packed, but approximately spherical when isolated from their neighbours. They have large central vacuoles, which allows the cells to store and regulate ions, waste products and water.

Parenchyma cells have a variety of functions:

- In leaves, they form the mesophyll and are responsible for photosynthesis and the exchange of gases.
- Storage of starch, protein, fats and oils and water in roots, tubers (e.g. potato), seed endosperm (e.g. cereals) and cotyledons (e.g. pulses and groundnut)
- Secretion (e.g. hydathodes, nectaries and cells lining the inside of resin ducts)
- Wound repair and the potential for renewed meristematic activity
- Other specialized functions such as aeration (aerenchyma) and support

The form of parenchyma cells varies with their function. The epidermal parenchyma cells of a leaf are barrel shaped in cross section, but have a variety of outline shapes ranging from simple polygons to strongly branched and interlocked shapes resembling the pieces of a jigsaw puzzle, as in the leaves of *Arabidopsis thaliana*. In the epidermis of higher plants, only the guard cells have chloroplasts. This tissue serves as a barrier wall and protects the internal tissues from injury the spongy mesophyll of a leaf, parenchyma cells range from near-spherical and loosely arranged with large intercellular spaces to branched or stellate, mutally interconnected with their neighbours at the ends of the arms to form a three-dimensional network, as in the red kidney bean *Phaseolus vulgaris* and other mesophytes. These cells, with the epidermal guard cells of the stoma, form a system of air spaces and chambers that regulate the exchange of gases

Collenchyma

The name 'collenchyma' derives from the Greek word "kolla", meaning "glue", which refers to the thick, glistening appearance of the walls in fresh tissues. Collenchyma tissue is composed of elongated cells with unevenly thickened walls. They provide structural support, particularly in growing shoots and leaves. Collenchyma tissue composes, for example, the resilient strands in stalks of celery. Its growth is strongly affected by mechanical stress upon the plant. The walls of collenchyma in shaken plants (to mimic the effects of wind etc), may be 40%-100% thicker than those not shaken. The wall is made up of cellulose and pectin.

There are three principal types of collenchyma:

- Angular collenchyma (thickened at intercellular contact points)
- Tangential collenchyma (cells arranged into ordered rows and thickened at the tangential face of the cell wall)
- Lacunar collenchyma (have intercellular space and thickening proximal to the intercellular space)

Collenchyma cells are most often found adjacent to outer growing tissues, the vascular cambium.

Sclerenchyma

Sclerenchyma is a supporting tissue. Two groups of sclerenchyma cells exist: fibres and sclereids. Their walls consist of cellulose, hemicellulose and lignin. Sclerenchyma cells are the principal supporting cells in plant tissues that have ceased elongation. Sclerenchyma fibres are of great economical importance, since they constitute the source material for many fabrics (flax, hemp, jute, ramie).

Unlike the collenchyma, mature sclerenchyma is composed of dead cells with extremely thick cell walls (secondary walls) that make up to 90% of the whole cell volume. The term "sclerenchyma" is derived from the Greek "scleros", meaning "hard". It is the hard, thick walls that make sclerenchyma cells important strengthening and supporting elements in plant parts that have ceased elongation. The difference between fibres and sclereids is not always clear. Transitions do exist, sometimes even within one and the same plant.

Fibres or bast are generally long, slender, so-called prosenchymatous cells, usually occurring in strands or bundles. Such bundles or the totality of a stem's bundles are colloquially called fibres. Their high load-bearing capacity and the ease with which they can be processed has since antiquity made them the source material for a number of things, like ropes, fabrics or mattresses. The fibres of flax (*Linum usitatissimum*) have been known in Europe and Egypt for more than 3000 years, those of hemp (*Cannabis sativa*) in China for just as long. These fibres, and those of jute (*Corchorus capsularis*) and ramie (*Boehmeria nivea*, a nettle), are extremely soft and elastic and are especially well suited for the processing to textiles. Their principal cell wall material is cellulose.

Contrasting are hard fibres that are mostly found in monocots. Typical examples are the fibres of many Gramineae, Agaves (sisal: *Agave sisalana*), lilies (*Yucca* or *Phormium tenax*), *Musa textilis* and others. Their cell walls contain, besides cellulose, a high proportion of lignin. The load-bearing capacity of *Phormium tenax* is as high as 20-25 kg/mm^2, the same as that of good steel wire (25 kg/mm^2), but the fibre tears as soon as too great a strain is placed upon it, while the wire distorts and does not tear before a strain of 80 kg/mm^2. The thickening of a cell wall has been studied in *Linum*. Starting at the centre of the fibre are the thickening layers of the secondary wall deposited one after the other. Growth at both tips of the cell leads to simultaneous elongation. During development the layers of secondary material seem like tubes, of which the outer one is always longer and older than the next. After completion of growth the missing parts are supplemented, so that the wall is evenly thickened up to the tips of the fibres.

Fibres usually originate from meristematic tissues. Cambium and procambium are their main centers of production. They are usually associated with the xylem and phloem of the vascular bundles. The fibres of the xylem are always lignified, while those of the phloem are cellulosic. Reliable evidence for the fibre cells' evolutionary origin from tracheids exists. During evolution the strength of the tracheid cell walls was enhanced, the ability to conduct water was lost and the size of the pits reduced. Fibres that do not belong to the xylem are bast (outside the ring of cambium) and such fibres that are arranged in characteristic patterns at different sites of the shoot.

Sclereids are small bundles of sclerenchyma tissue in plants that form durable layers, such as the cores of apples and the gritty texture of pears. Sclereids are variable in shape. The cells can be isodiametric, prosenchymatic, forked or elaborately branched. They can be grouped into bundles, can form complete tubes located at the periphery or can occur as single cells or small groups of cells within parenchyma tissues. But compared with most fibres, sclereids are relatively short. Characteristic examples are the stone cells (called stone cells because of their hardness) of pears (*Pyrus communis*) and quinces (*Cydonia oblonga*) and those of the shoot of the wax-plant (*Hoya carnosa*). The cell walls fill nearly all the cell's volume. A layering of the walls and the existence of branched pits is clearly visible. Branched pits such as these are called ramiform pits. The shell of many seeds like those of nuts as well as the stones of drupes like cherries or plums are made up from sclereids.

VASCULAR TISSUE

Vascular tissue is a complex tissue found in vascular plants, meaning that it is composed of more than one cell type. The primary components of vascular tissue are the xylem and phloem. These two tissues transport fluid and nutrients internally. There are also two meristems associated with vascular tissue: the vascular cambium and the cork cambium. All the vascular tissues within a particular plant together constitute the vascular tissue system of that plant.

The cells in differentiated vascular tissue are typically long and slender. Since the xylem and phloem function in the conduction of water, minerals, and nutrients throughout the plant, it is not surprising that their form should be similar to pipes. The individual cells of phloem are connected end-to-end, just as the sections of a pipe might be. As the plant grows, new vascular tissue differentiates in the growing tips of the plant. The new tissue is aligned with existing vascular tissue, maintaining its connection throughout the plant. The vascular tissue in plants is arranged in long, discrete strands called vascular bundles. These bundles include both xylem and phloem, as well as supporting and protective cells. In stems and roots, the xylem typically lies closer to the interior of the stem with phloem towards the exterior of the stem. In the stems of some Asteriidae dicots, there may be phloem located inwardly from the xylem as well.

Between the xylem and phloem is a meristem called the vascular cambium. This tissue divides off cells that will be become additional xylem and phloem. This growth increases the girth of the plant, rather than its length. As long as the vascular cambium continues to produce new cells, the plant will continue to grow more stout. In trees and other plants that develop wood, the vascular cambium allows the expansion of vascular tissue that produces woody growth. Because this growth ruptures the epidermis of the stem, woody plants also have a cork cambium that develops among the phloem. The cork cambium gives rise to thickened cork cells to protect the surface of the plant and reduce water loss. Both the production of wood and the production of cork are forms of secondary growth.

In leaves, the vascular bundles are located among the spongy mesophyll. The xylem is oriented toward the adaxial surface of the leaf (usually the upper side), and phloem is oriented toward the abaxial surface of the leaf. This is why aphids are typically found on the underside of the leaves rather than on the top, since the phloem transports sugars manufactured by the plant and they are closer to the lower surface.

CHAPTER 6

Tree Roots

INTRODUCTION

In vascular plants, the root is the organ of a plant body that typically lies below the surface of the soil. But, this is not always the case, since a root can also be aerial (that is, growing above the ground) or aerating (that is, growing up above the ground or especially above water). On the other hand, a stem normally occurring below ground is not exceptional either (see rhizome). So, it is better to define *root* as a part of a plant body that bears no leaves, and therefore also lacks nodes. There are also important internal structural differences between stems and roots. The two major functions of roots are: (1) absorption of water and inorganic nutrients; and (2) anchoring the plant body to the ground. Roots also function in cytokinin synthesis, which supplies some of the shoot's needs. They often function in storage of food. The roots of most vascular plant species enter into symbiosis with certain fungi to form mycorrhizas, and a large range of other organisms including bacteria also closely associate with roots.

At the tip of every growing root is a conical covering of tissue called the root cap, which consists of undifferentiated soft tissue (parenchyma) with unthickened walls covering the apical meristem. The root cap provides mechanical protection to the meristem as the root advances through the soil. As the root cap cells are worn away they are continually replaced by new cells generated by cell division within the meristem. The root cap is also involved in the production of mucigel, a sticky mucilage that coats the new formed cells. These cells contain statoliths, starch grains that move in response to gravity and thus control root orientation.

The outside surface of the primary root is the epidermis. Recently produced *epidermal* cells absorb water from the surrounding environment and produce outgrowths called root hairs that greatly increase the cell's absorptive surface. Root hairs are very delicate and generally short-lived, remaining functional for only a few days. However, as the root grows, new epidermal cells emerge and these form new root hairs, replacing those that die. The process by which water is absorbed into the epidermal cells from the soil is known as *osmosis*. For this reason, water that is saline is more difficult for most plant species to absorb.

Beneath the epidermis is the cortex, which comprises the bulk of the primary root. Its main function is storage of starch. Intercellular spaces in the cortex aerate cells for respiration. An endodermis is a thin layer of small cells forming the innermost part of the cortex and surrounding the vascular tissues deeper in the root. The tightly packed cells of the endodermis contain a substance known as suberin in their cell walls. This suberin layer is the Casparian strip, which creates an impermeable barrier of sorts. Mineral nutrients can only move passively within root cell walls until they reach the endodermis. At that point, they must be actively transported across a cell membrane to continue further into the root. This allows the plant to accumulate mineral nutrients in the stele.

The vascular cylinder, or stele, consists of the cells inside the endodermis. The outer part, known as the pericycle, surrounds the actual vascular tissue. In monocotyledonous plants, the xylem and phloem cells are arranged in a circle around a pith or center, whereas in dicotyledons, the xylem cells form a central "hub" with lobes, and phloem cells fill in the spaces between the lobes.

Secondary Growth

All roots have primary growth or growth in length. Roots of many vascular plants, especially dicots and gymnosperms, often undergo secondary growth, which is an increase in diameter. A vascular cambium forms in the stele to produce secondary phloem and secondary xylem. The epidermis is replaced by a periderm. As the stele increases in diameter, the cortex, pericycle and endodermis are lost. Even non-woody roots often undergo secondary growth, including those of tomato and alfalfa.

ROOT GROWTH

Early root growth is one of the functions of the apical meristem located near the tip of the root. The meristem cells more or less continuously divide, producing more meristem, root cap cells (these are sacrificed to protect the meristem), and undifferentiated root cells. The latter will become the primary tissues of the root, first undergoing elongation, a process that pushes the root tip forward in the growing medium. Gradually these cells differentiate and mature into specialized cells of the root tissues.

Roots will generally grow in any direction where the correct environment of air, mineral nutrients and water exists to meet the plant's needs. Roots will not grow in dry soil. Over time, given the right conditions, roots can crack foundations, snap water lines, and lift sidewalks. At germination, roots grow downward due to gravitropism, the growth mechanism of plants that also causes the shoot to grow upward. In some plants (such as ivy), the "root" actually clings to walls and structures.

Growth from apical meristems is known as primary growth, which encompasses all elongation. Secondary growth encompasses all growth in diameter, a major component of woody plant tissues and many nonwoody plants. For example, storage roots of sweet potato have secondary growth but are not woody. Secondary growth occurs at the lateral meristems, namely the vascular cambium and cork cambium. The former forms secondary xylem and secondary phloem, while the latter forms the periderm.

In plants with secondary growth, the vascular cambium, originating between the xylem and the phloem, forms a cylinder of tissue along the stem and root. The cambium layer forms new cells on both the inside and outside of the cambium cylinder, with those on the inside forming secondary xylem cells, and those on the outside forming secondary phloem cells. As secondary xylem accumulates, the "girth" (lateral dimensions) of the stem and root increases. As a result, tissues beyond the secondary phloem (including the epidermis and cortex, in many cases) tend to be pushed outward and are eventually "sloughed off" (shed).

At this point, the cork cambium begins to form the periderm, consisting of protective cork cells containing suberin. In roots, the cork cambium originates in the pericycle, a component of the vascular cylinder.

Stilt roots in the Amazon Rainforest support a tree in very soft, wet soil conditions.

The vascular cambium produces new layers of secondary xylem annually. The xylem vessels are dead at maturity but are responsible for most water transport through the vascular tissue in stems and roots.

TYPES OF ROOTS

A true root system consists of a primary root and secondary roots (or lateral roots). The primary root originates in the radicle of the seedling. It is the first part of the root to be originated. During its growth it rebranches to form the lateral roots. It usually grows downwards. Generally, two categories are recognized:

- the taproot system: the primary root is prominent and has a single, dominant axis; there are fibrous secondary roots running outward. Usually allows for deeper roots capable of reaching low water tables. Most common in dicots. The main function of the taproot is to store food.
- the diffuse root system: the primary root is not dominant; the whole root system is fibrous and branches in all directions. Most common in monocots. The main function of the fibrous root is to anchor the plant.

Specialized Roots

The roots, or parts of roots, of many plant species have become specialized to serve adaptive purposes besides the two primary functions described in the introduction.

- *Adventitious roots* arise out-of-sequence from the more usual root formation of branches of a primary root, and instead originate from the stem, branches, leaves, or old woody roots. They commonly occur in monocots and pteridophytes, but also in many dicots, such as clover (*Trifolium*), ivy (*Hedera*), strawberry (*Fragaria*) and willow (*Salix*). Most aerial roots and stilt roots are adventitious. In some conifers adventitious roots can form the largest part of the root system.
- *Aerating roots* (or *pneumatophores*): roots rising above the ground, especially above water such as in some mangrove genera (*Avicennia, Sonneratia*). In some plants like *Avicennia* the erect roots have a large number of breathing pores for exchange of gases.
- *Aerial roots:* roots entirely above the ground, such as in ivy (*Hedera*) or in epiphytic orchids. They function as prop roots.
- *Contractile roots:* they pull bulbs or corms of monocots, such as hyacinth and lily, and some taproots, such as dandelion, deeper in the soil through expanding radially and contracting longitudinally. They have a wrinkled surface.
- *Coarse roots:* Roots that have undergone secondary thickening and have a woody structure. These roots have some ability to absorb water and nutrients, but their main function is transport and to provide a structure to connect the smaller diameter, fine roots to the rest of the plant.
- *Fine roots:* Primary roots usually <2 mm diameter that have the function of water and nutrient uptake. They are often heavily branched and support mycorrhizas. These roots may be short lived, but are replaced by the plant in an ongoing process of root 'turnover'.

- *Haustorial roots:* roots of parasitic plants that can absorb water and nutrients from another plant, such as in mistletoe (*Viscum album*) and dodder.
- *Propagative roots:* roots that form adventitious buds that develop into aboveground shoots, termed suckers, which form new plants, as in Canada thistle, cherry and many others.
- *Proteoid roots* or cluster roots: dense clusters of rootlets of limited growth that develop under low phosphate or low iron conditions in Proteaceae and some plants from the following families Betulaceae, Casuarinaceae, Eleagnaceae, Moraceae, Fabaceae and Myricaceae.
- *Stilt roots:* these are adventitious support roots, common among mangroves. They grow down from lateral branches, branching in the soil.
- *Storage roots:* these roots are modified for storage of food or water, such as carrots and beets. They include some taproots and tuberous roots.
- *Structural roots:* large roots that have undergone considerable secondary thickening and provide mechanical support to woody plants and trees.
- *Surface roots:* These proliferate close below the soil surface, exploiting water and easily available nutrients. Where conditions are close to optimum in the surface layers of soil, the growth of surface roots is encouraged and they commonly become the dominant roots.
- *Tuberous roots:* A portion of a root swells for food or water storage, e.g. sweet potato. A type of storage root distinct from taproot.

Rooting Depths

The distribution of vascular plant roots within soil depends on plant form, the spatial and temporal availability of water and nutrients, and the physical properties of the soil. The deepest roots are generally found in deserts and temperate coniferous forests; the shallowest in tundra, boreal forest and temperate grasslands.

The deepest observed living root, at least 60 m below the ground surface, was observed during the excavation of an open-pit mine in Arizona, USA. Some roots can grow as deep as the tree is high. The majority of roots on most plants are however found relatively close to the surface where nutrient availability and aeration are more favourable for growth. Rooting depth may be physically restricted by rock or compacted soil close below the surface, or by anaerobic soil conditions.

The pattern of development of a root system is termed 'root architecture', and is important in providing a plant with a secure supply of nutrients and water as well as anchorage and support. The architecture of a root system can be considered in a similar way to above-ground architecture of a plant - i.e. in terms of the size, branching and distribution of the component parts. In roots, the architecture of fine roots and coarse roots can both be described by variation in topology and distribution of biomass within and between roots. Having a balanced architecture allows fine roots to exploit soil efficiently around a plant, but the 'plastic' nature of root growth allows the plant to then concentrate its resources where nutrients and water are more easily available. A balanced coarse root architecture, with roots distributed relatively evenly around the stem base, is necessary to provide support to larger plants and trees.

ECONOMIC IMPORTANCE

Roots can also protect the environment by holding the soil to prevent soil erosion.

The term root crops refers to any edible underground plant structure, but many root crops are actually stems, such as potato tubers. Edible roots include cassava, sweet potato, beet, carrot, rutabaga, turnip, parsnip, radish, yam and horseradish. Spices obtained from roots include sassafras, angelica, sarsaparilla and licorice.

Sugar beet is an important source of sugar. Yam roots are a source of estrogen compounds used in birth control pills. The fish poison and insecticide rotenone is obtained from roots of *Lonchocarpus* spp. Important medicines from roots are ginseng, aconite, ipecac, gentian and reserpine. Several legumes that have nitrogen-fixing root nodules are used as green manure crops, which provide nitrogen fertilizer for other crops when plowed under. Specialized bald cypress roots, termed knees, are sold as souvenirs, lamp bases and carved into folk art. Native Americans used the flexible roots of white spruce for basketry.

Tree roots can heave and destroy concrete sidewalks and crush or clog buried pipes. The aerial roots of strangler fig have damaged ancient Mayan temples in Central America and the temple of Angkor Wat in Cambodia.

Vegetative propagation of plants via cuttings depends on adventitious root formation. Hundreds of millions of plants are propagated via cuttings annually including chrysanthemum, poinsettia, carnation, ornamental shrubs and many houseplants.

Roots can also protect the environment by holding the soil to prevent soil erosion.

STOLON

Stolons are horizontal stems which grow at the soil surface or below ground. They form new plants at the ends or at the nodes. Stolons are often called runners. Imprecisely they are stems that run atop or just under the ground; more specifically, a stolon is a horizontal shoot from a plant that grows on top of or below the soil surface with the ability to produce new clones of the same plant from buds at the tip.

Stolons are similar to normal stems except they produce adventitious roots at the nodes and run horizontally rather than vertically. They also have long internodes with reduced leaves, with the exception of stolons in aqueous plants. Plants with stolons or stolon-like rhizomes are called stoloniferous. A stolon is a plant propagation strategy and the complex of individuals formed by a mother plant and all its clones produced from stolons form a single genetic individual. Runners are a type of stolon that exist above ground and are produced by many plants, such as strawberries. Stolons lack the same type of reduced leaves that rhizomes have at the nodes; stolons have scale-like leaves and new roots are formed at the nodes only while rhizomes typically have paper like leaves at the nodes. Typically, stolons have very long internodes that form new plants at the ends. These rise to the soil surface and can produce foliage and flowers. In contrast, rhizomes most often have short internodes with leaf-scars and thin paper-like leaves and root along the under side of the stem. Root formation does not correspond strictly to the nodes but roots can generate from areas around the scar-like nodes as well.

Stolons are like long branches of a tree that grow horizontal to the soil surface and produce new plants at the ends, they have nodes and internodes, leaves that are reduced to scales and buds that grow into roots and shoots. Stolons arise from the base of the plant in strawberries the base is above the soil surface, in many bulb-forming species and plants with rhizomes under ground and remain underground and form shoots that rise to the surface at the ends or from the nodes. The nodes of the stolons produce roots, often all around the node and hormones produced by the roots cause the stolon to initiate shoots with normal leaves. Typically after the formation of the new plant the stolon dies away in a year or two, while rhizomes persist normally for many years or for the life of the plant, adding more length each year to the ends with active growth. Rhizomes are used as storage structures for nutrients and most often are covered with thin papery leaves (normally a translucent brownish color), while stolons are not covered with reduced leaves but have scales like leaves at the nodes that are most often white in color. Stolons look and act like etiolated stems except for their orientation of growth, instead of stretching upward for light they grow laterally or downward. The horizontal growth of stolons results from the interplay of different hormones produced at the growing point and hormones from the main plant, with some studies showing that stolon and rhizome growth effected by the amount of shady light the plant receives with increased production and branching from plants exposed to mixed shade and sun, while plants in all day sun or all shade producing fewer stolons.

Often the general meaning of stolon (horizontal stems above ground) does not distinguish morphologically the differences between stolons and rhizomes but just differentiates rhizome and stolon from each other strictly by where they are found, with rhizomes being below ground. Though this generalization is imprecise with a number of plants having soil level or above ground rhizomes including *Iris* species and many orchid species. Because of this some botany texts now use the term underground stolon to refer to stolons that move under ground.

T. Holm (1929) restricted the term rhizome to a horizontal, usually subterranean, stem that produces roots from its lower surface and green leaves from its apex, developed directly from the plumule of the embryo. He recognized stolons as axillary, subterranean branches that do not bear green leaves but only membranaceous, scale-like ones.

Lipstick Strawberry (*Potentilla palustrix* × *Fragaria* × *ananassa*) along stolons.

In some *Cyperus* species the stolons end with the growth of tubers; the tubers are swollen stolons that form new plants.

Some species of crawling plants can also sprout adventitious roots, but are not considered stoloniferous: a stolon is sprouted from an existing stem and can produce a full individual. Examples of plants that extend through stolons include some species from the genera *Argentina* (silverweed), *Cynodon*, *Fragaria*, and *Pilosella* (Hawkweeds), *Zoysia japonica*, *Ranunculus repens*. Other plants with stolons below the soil surface include many grasses, *Ajuga*, *Mentha*, and *Stachys*.

Lily-of-the-valley (*Convallaria majalis*) which has rhizomes that grow stolon-like stems called stoloniferous rhizomes or leptomorph rhizomes. A number of plants have stoloniferous rhizomes including Asters These stolon-like rhizomes are long and thin, with long internodes and indeterminate growth with lateral buds at the node that mostly remain dormant.

In potatoes, the stolons start to grow within 10 days of plants emerging above ground, with tubers usually beginning to form on the end of the stolons. The tubers are modified stolons that hold food reserves with a few buds that grow into stems. Since it is *not* a rhizome it does not generate roots, but the new stem growth that grows to the surface produces roots. See also BBCH-scale (potato).

Hydrilla use stolons that produce tubers to spread themselves and survive dry periods in aquatic habitats.

Erythronium commonly called Trout Lily, have white stolons growing from the bulb. Most run horizontally, either underground or along the surface of the ground under leaf litter. Flowering plants often produce no stolons. A number of bulbous forming species produce stolons with *Erythronium propullans* producing one stolon below the soil surface on the midway point of the stem on blooming plants that produces a new bulb. On non blooming plants 1 to 3 stolons are produce directly from the bulbs, each ending in a new clone.

Convolvulus arvensis is a weed species in agriculture that spreads by under ground stolons that produce rhizomes.

In studies on grass species, with plants that produce stolons or rhizomes and plants that produce both stolons and rhizomes; morphological and physiological differences where noticed. Stolons have longer internodes and function as means of seeking out light and were used for propagation of the plant, while rhizomes are used as storage organs for carbohydrates and the maintenance of meristem tissue to keep the parent plant alive from one year to the next

Mycology

In mycology, a stolon is defined as an occasionally septate hyphae, which connect sporangiophores together. Root-like structures called rhizoids may appear on the stolon as well, anchoring the hyphae to the substrate. The stolon is commonly found in bread molds, and are seen as horizontally expanding across the mold.

CUTTING (PLANT)

Plant cutting, also known as striking/cloning, is a technique for vegetatively (asexually) propagating plants in which a piece of the source plant containing at least one stem cell is placed in a suitable medium such as moist soil, potting mix, coir or rock wool. The cutting produces new roots, stems, or both, and thus becomes a new plant independent of the parent.

Technique

Typically, striking is a simple process in which a small amount of the parent plant is removed. This removed piece, called the *cutting*, is then encouraged to grow as an independent plant.

However, to have a fair degree of success, the practice of taking cuttings is not as straightforward/easy as it may appear. If strikings are taken without providing the right growing conditions, it is more likely than not that the cutting will not "catch on" (form roots).

Thus, to have a fair amount of cuttings catching on, the cutting should have:

- good, moist soil; that is soil that is light/airy and which contains sufficient nutrients.
- a humid environment (this generally means placing the cuttings under a plastic sheet or in another confined space where through simple watering, the air can be kept humid/moist.
- partial shade (to prevent the cutting from drying out).

After cuttings are placed in soil, they are watered thoroughly with a fine mist. The fine mist of a nozzle sprayer or a spray mist bottle are often used. After the initial watering, soil is allowed to almost dry out before misting again, with the aim to keep the soil moist but not wet and waterlogged. A fine mist is used to avoid disturbing plants.

In addition, the cutting needs to be taken correctly; this means:

- at the right time; in temperate countries, stem cuttings of young wood need to be taken in spring, of hardened wood they need to be taken in winter.
- with the right size and amount of foliage; length of stem cuttings of soft wood for example need to be between 5-15cm and of hard wood between 20-25cm. Also, the foliage of soft wood stem cuttings needs to be removed by 2/3 and of hard wood stem cuttings, complete foliage removal is necessary.

Also, though not essential, several compounds may be used to promote the formation of roots such as the auxins. Among the commonly used ones is indole-3-butyric acid, or IBA, used as a powder, solution or gel. This compound is applied either to the cut tip of the cutting or as a foliar spray.

Types of Cuttings

Many vegetative parts of a plant can be used. The most common methods are:

- Stem cuttings, in which a piece of stem is part buried in the soil, including at least one leaf node. It produces new roots, usually at the node.
- Root cuttings, in which a section of root is buried just below the soil surface, and produces new shoots.
- Scion cuttings; which are dormant 'ligneous' woody twigs.
- Eye cuttings, which are pieces of foliated or defoliated stalks with one or more eyes.
- Leaf cuttings, in which a leaf is placed on moist soil. These have to develop both new stems and new roots. Some leaves will produce one plant at the base of the leaf. In some species, multiple new plants can be produced at many places on one leaf, and these can be induced by cutting the leaf veins.

Although some species, such as willow, blackberry and pelargoniums can be struck simply by sticking into moist ground, most species require more attention. Most species, require humid, warm, partially shaded conditions to strike, thus requiring the approach above to be followed. Particularly difficult species may need cool air above and warm soil. In addition, with many more difficult strikings, one would also prefer to use the type of cutting that has the most chance of success with that particular plant species.

Providing the Right Soil

Depending on the type of soil with which you start, several additives may need adding to create good soil for cuttings. These additions may include:

- chalk; to increase the pH-value of the soil; a Ph of 6-6, 5 is to be maintained;
- organic substance/humus; to increase nutrient load; keep to a bare minimum though;
- sand/gravel; to increase the soil's water permeability.

For example with plain potting soil, you would want to add 1/3 sand to make suitable soil for cuttings.

Providing the Right Humidity

A white plastic greenhouse, used to keep the cuttings humid

Although several options can be used here, usually semi-white plastic is used to cover the cuttings. The soil below and from the cuttings themselves is kept moist. Aerate once in a while to prevent formation of molds.

Rooting Substance

As mentioned before, rooting hormone may be used to facilitate striking, yet is generally not the most important factor in the process. However it is helpful with especially hard plant species.

Many root promoting products from various companies are offered on the market. Substances with rooting effects are almost inevitably based on signaling activity of plant hormone auxin and various auxin compounds (IAA, NAA, IBA, ..) were implemented in various commercially available products. If you do not want to buy similar product on market, you may try prepare some rooting substance in more traditional way.

Making your Own Rooting Hormone

- When starting a new plant from a leaf or stem cutting, the cutting will be more likely to form roots and create a new plant if a rooting hormone is used.
- While commercial rooting hormone can be used there are organic homemade versions that work as well.
- To make rooting hormone, soak the yellow-tipped shoots of a weeping willow tree in water. A tea made from the bark

of a willow tree is also effective. When using the shoots or bark, soak them for 24 hours prior to using.

- Some people have found that using honey makes an effective rooting hormone as well.

Leaf cuttings: Any plant with leaves such as African Violet, Geranium etc. can be propagated with leaf cuttings. Using a sharp knife, cut off a healthy leaf at the point where it joins the stem. Insert the cut part, called a petiole, into the rooting hormone. Place the end into a small container of light potting soil in which you make a small hole with a pencil.

Making a hole prior to planting assures that the rooting hormone will not be brushed off the cutting when you plant it. Perlite, Vermiculite, and/or water-soaked Sphagnum moss can be added to potting soil to make the soil light. Make sure the leaf is leaning slightly so that the new plants will have plenty of light and not be shaded by the leaf.

Stem cuttings: These are treated just like leaf cuttings except you cut off a stem with several leaves instead of just one leaf. Remove the bottom leaves, leaving a few at the top. Proceed as with the leaf cutting.

In both instances, cover the pot with a plastic bag or inverted glass jar. This will keep moisture from evaporating and keep the cutting from wilting. Keep in a warm location with diffused light but out of direct sunlight. When there is indications of growth after about 3 to 6 weeks, transplant the new emerging plant into a new pot of potting soil. Continue to keep a humid environment for about 2 more weeks until active growth begins.

In temperate countries, stem cuttings may be taken of soft (green or semi-ripe) wood and hard wood which has specific differences in practice. Stem cuttings of soft wood is taken in spring, while from hard wood, they are taken in winter. Also, of soft wood the upper branches are taken (with a length of 5-15cm) and with hard wood, the lower branches are taken instead (with a length of 20-25 cm). Finally, soft wood cuttings are planted above ground and hard wood cuttings are totally submerged with soil. With hard wood cuttings, several cuttings are also bound together (to a bushel).

Grafting

Grafting is a method of asexual plant propagation widely used in agriculture and horticulture where the tissues of one plant are encouraged to fuse with those of another. It is most commonly used for the propagation of trees and shrubs grown commercially. (Grafting is limited to dicots and gymnosperms. Monocots lack the vascular cambium required.)

In most cases, one plant is selected for its roots, and this is called the *stock* or rootstock. The other plant is selected for its stems, leaves, flowers, or fruits and is called the *scion*. The scion contains the desired genes to be duplicated in future production by the stock/scion plant.

In stem grafting, a common grafting method, a shoot of a selected, desired plant cultivar is grafted onto the stock of another type. In another common form called budding, a dormant side bud is grafted on the stem of another stock plant, and when it has fused successfully, it is encouraged to grow by cutting out the stem above the new bud.

For successful grafting to take place, the vascular cambium tissues of the stock and scion plants must be placed in contact with each other. Both tissues must be kept alive until the graft has taken, usually a period of a few weeks. Successful grafting only requires that a vascular connection takes place between the two tissues. A physical weak point often still occurs at the graft, because the structural tissue of the two distinct plants, such as wood may not fuse.

Reasons for Grafting

- *Dwarfing:* To induce dwarfing or cold tolerance or other characteristics to the scion. Most apple trees in modern orchards are grafted dwarf or semi-dwarf trees planted at high density. They provide more fruit per unit of land, higher quality fruit, and reduce the danger of accidents by harvest crews working on ladders.
- *Ease of propagation:* Because the scion is difficult to propagate vegetatively by other means, such as by cuttings. In this case, cuttings of an easily rooted plant are used to

provide a rootstock. In some cases, the scion may be easily propagated, but grafting may still be used because it is commercially the most cost-effective way of raising a particular type of plant.

- *Hybrid breeding:* To speed maturity of hybrids in fruit tree breeding programmes. Hybrid seedlings may take ten or more years to flower and fruit on their own roots. Grafting can reduce the time to flowering and shorten the breeding programme.
- *Hardiness:* Because the scion has weak roots or the roots of the stock plants have roots tolerant of difficult conditions. e.g. many showy Western Australian plants are sensitive to dieback on heavy soils, common in urban gardens, and are grafted onto hardier eastern Australian relatives. Grevilleas and eucalypts are examples.
- *Sturdiness* In order to provide a strong, tall trunk for certain ornamental shrubs and trees. In these cases, a graft is made at a desired height on a stock plant with a strong stem. This is used to raise 'standard' roses, which are rose bushes on a high stem, and it is also used for some ornamental trees, such as certain weeping cherries.
- *Pollen source:* To provide pollenizers. For example, in tightly planted or badly planned apple orchards of a single variety, limbs of crab apple may be grafted at regularly spaced intervals onto trees down rows, say every fourth tree. This takes care of pollen needs at blossom time, yet does not confuse pickers who might otherwise mix varieties while harvesting, as the mature crab apples are so distinct from other apple varieties.
- *Repair:* To repair damage to the trunk of a tree which would prohibit nutrient flow, such as the stripping of the bark by rodents which completely girdles the trunk. In this case a bridge graft may be used to connect the tissues receiving flow from the roots to the tissues above the damage which have been severed from the flow. Where a watersprout, sucker or sapling of the same species is growing nearby, any

of these can be grafted to the area above the damage by a method called inarch grafting. These alternatives to scions must be of the correct length to span the gap of the wound.

- *Changing cultivars:* To change the cultivar in a fruit orchard to a more profitable cultivar, called *topworking*. It may be faster to graft a new cultivar onto existing limbs of established trees than to replant an entire orchard.
- *Maintain consistency:* Apples are notorious for their genetic variability, even differing in multiple characteristics, such as, size, color, and flavor, of fruits located on the same tree. In the commercial farming industry, consistency is maintained by grafting a scion with desired fruit traits onto a hardy stock.

Curiosities

- A practice sometimes carried out by gardeners is to graft related potatoes and tomatoes so that both are produced on the same plant, one above ground and one underground.
- Cacti of widely different forms are sometimes grafted on to each other.
- Multiple cultivars of fruits such as apples are sometimes grafted on a single tree. This so-called "family tree" provides more fruit variety for small spaces such as a suburban backyard, and also takes care of the need for pollenizers. The drawback is that the gardener must be sufficiently trained to prune them correctly, or one strong variety will usually "take over". Occasionally, a so-called "graft hybrid" or "chimaera" can occur where the tissues of the stock continue to grow within the scion. Such a plant can produce flowers and foliage typical of both plants as well as shoots intermediate between the two. The best-known example is probably +*Laburnocytisus* 'Adamii', a graft hybrid between laburnum and broom, which originated in a nursery near Paris, France in 1825. This small tree bears yellow flowers typical of *Laburnum anagyroides*, purple flowers typical of *Chamaecytisus purpureus* and curious coppery-pink flowers which show characteristics of both "parents".

- Ornamental and functional, arborsculpture uses grafting techniques to join separate trees or parts of the same tree to itself. Furniture, hearts, entry archways are examples. Axel Erlandson was a prolific arborsculptor growing over 75 mature shaped and grafted trees.

The easiest and most common form of grafting is cleft grafting. The stock is simply split and the scion is inserted. It is best if the stock is 2-7 cm in diameter and has 3-5 buds, and the cleft is around 7cm deep. The scion is cut in a wedge shape and inserted into the tree with the cambium. The bare stock is covered with grafting compound, otherwise the cambium layer quickly dries and the graft fails.

Stub

Stub grafting is a technique that requires less stock than cleft grafting, and retains the shape of a tree. Also scions are generally of 6-8 buds in this process. An incision is made into the branch one centimetere long, then the scion is wedged and forced into the branch. The scion should be at an angle of at most 35° to the parent tree so that the crotch remains strong. The graft is covered with grafting compound.

Awl

Awl grafting takes the least resources and the least time must is best done by an experienced grafter for fear that the grafter would accidentally drive his tool too far into the stock and then the scion would have a reduced chance of survival. Awl grafting can be done by using a screwdriver to make a slit in the bark but just so far as the cambium layer. Then inset the wedged scion into the incision.

Veneer

Veneer grafting, or inlay grafting, is a method used for stocks larger than three centimeters in diameter. The scion is recommended to be about as thick as a pencil. Clefts are made of the same size as the scion on the side of the branch, not on top. The scion end is shaped as a wedge, inserted, and wrapped with tape to the scaffolding branches to give it more strength.

Renewing Fusion

"Renewing fusion" is a grafting method in which a small branch (at least a centimeter wide) from one plant to a main branch of another, by carefully shaving a proper amount of bark from the large branch and inserting the scion into a cut hole. The graft is taped with a thin strip of duct tape in diagonal lashings, to hold it up and to prevent insects from entering the hole. The origin of grafting is uncertain. the peoples of ancient civilizations who grew fruit trees may have observed natural unions made by twigs and branches of compatible trees growing next to one another.

Natural Grafting

Tree roots of the same species will sometimes naturally graft where they make physical contact with each other. A group of trees can share water and mineral nutrients via root grafts, which may be advantageous to weaker trees, and may also form a larger rootmass as an adaptation to promote fire resistence and regeneration as exemplified by the California Black Oak. A problem with root grafts is that they allow transmission of certain pathogens, such as Dutch elm disease. Natural grafting also sometimes occurs where two stems on the same tree, shrub or vine make contact with each other. This is common in plants such as strawberries and potatoes.

Scientific Uses

Grafting has been important in flowering research. Leaves or shoots from plants induced to flower can be grafted onto uninduced plants and transmit a floral stimulus that induces them to flower. The transmission of plant viruses has been studied using grafting. Virus indexing involves grafting a symptom-less plant that is suspected of carrying a virus onto an indicator plant that is very susceptible to the virus.

Herbaceous Grafting

Grafting is often done for non-woody plants such as a tomato, cucumber, eggplant and watermelon The main advantage of grafting is for disease-resistant rootstocks. In Japan there is an automated process using grafting robots.

Fruit Tree Propagation

Fruit tree propagation is usually carried out through asexual reproduction by grafting or budding the desired variety onto a suitable rootstock. Perennial plants can be propagated either by sexual or vegetative means. Sexual reproduction occurs when male pollen from one tree fertilises the ovules (incipient seeds) of the flower of another, stimulating the development of fruit. In turn this fruit contains a seed or seeds which, when germinated, will become a new specimen. However, the new tree will inherit many of the characteristics of both its parents, and it will not grow 'true' to the variety from which it came. That is, it will be a fresh individual with many unpredictable characteristics of its own. Although this is desirable in terms of increasing biodiversity and the richness of the gene pool (such sexual recombination is the source of most new cultivars), only rarely will such fruit trees be directly useful or attractive to the tastes of humankind. A tendency to revert to a wild-like state is common.

Therefore, from the orchard grower or gardener's point of view, it is preferable to propagate fruit cultivars vegetatively in order to ensure reliability. This involves taking a cutting (or scion) of wood from a desirable parent tree which is then grown on to produce a new plant or 'clone' of the original. In effect this means that the original Bramley apple tree, for example, was a successful variety grown from a pip, but that every Bramley since then has been propagated by taking cuttings of living matter from that tree, or one of its descendants.

Methods

The essentials of our present methods of propagating of fruit trees date from pre-Classical times. Grafting as a technique was first developed in China from where it was imported to Greece and Rome. Classical authors wrote extensively about the technical skills of fruit cultivation, including grafting techniques and rootstock selection. The oldest surviving named varieties of fruits date from classical times.

The simplest method of propagating a tree asexually is rooting. A cutting (a piece of the parent plant) is cut and stuck into soil. Artificial rooting hormones are sometimes used to assure success. If the cutting does not die of desiccation first, roots grow from the buried portion of the cutting to become a complete plant. Though this works well for some plants (such as figs and olives), most fruit trees are unsuited to this method.

Root cuttings (pieces of root induced to grow a new trunk) are used with some kinds of plants. This method also is suitable only for some plants. A refinement on rooting is layering. This is rooting a piece of a wood that is still attached to its parent and continues to receive nourishment from it. The new plant is severed only after it has successfully grown roots. Layering is the technique most used for propagation of clonal apple rootstocks.

The most common method of propagating fruit trees, suitable for nearly all species, is grafting onto rootstocks. These are varieties selected for characteristics such as their vigour of growth, hardiness, soil tolerance, and compatibility with the desired variety that will form the aerial part of the plant (called the scion). For example, grape rootstocks descended from North American grapes allow European grapes to be grown in areas infested with *Phylloxera*, a soil-dwelling insect that attacks and kills European grapes when grown on their own roots. Grafting is the process of joining these two varieties, ensuring maximum contact between the cambium tissue (that is, the layer of growing plant material just below the bark) of each so that they grow together successfully. Two of the most common grafting techniques are 'whip and tongue', carried out in spring as the sap rises, and 'budding', which is performed around July and August.

Another reason for grafting onto rootstocks is that this enables the grower to determine the tree's eventual size. Apple tree size classes number one to ten in increasing height and breadth. A "1" is a dwarf which can be productive and as short as three feet with proper pruning. A "10" is the standard sized tree with no dwarfing and will grow to twenty or more feet tall and wide, dependent upon the variety chosen. In general the class range is 10-20% of full size, 20-30%, 30-40% and so forth to size 10 which is 100% of full size.

Apple tree rootstocks are referred to by numbers prefixed by letters indicating the developer of the rootstock.

"M" designates Malling series developed stocks. East Malling Research is a pioneer in the development of dwarfing rootstocks. East Malling Research Station in Kent, England collected clones of the Paradise stocks from France in 1912 from which 24 "M" were designated with no particular order to the rootstock characteristics other than where they were located in the garden at the time the numbers were assigned. In other words, M.2 is larger tree than M.9 while M.27 is smaller than M.26.

"MM" designates Malling-Merton stocks developed from joint breeding programme by John Innes Institute, in Merton, England, & East Malling Research Station in the early 1950s The "MM" series was developed primarily to provide resistance to Woolly Apple Aphid(Eriosomatinae) infestation.

"EMLA" designates East Malling/Long Ashton research stations who took the "M" stocks and developed virus free versions. E.g., EMLA 7 is M 7 with a guaranteed virus free stock. EMLA characteristics are often different from the parent "M" rootstock. Note that nearly all the apple rootstocks in the industry are now virus free.

"CG" or *"G"* designates Cornell-Geneva stocks which are those developed via the Cornell & USDA collaboration at the New York Agricultural Experiment Station in Geneva, NY. The "G" is the old designation. All newer stocks are "CG" followed by numbers that actually provide some information about the stock.

- *M.27 Malling 27:* A very dwarfing rootstock. Unless the central leader is supported, the tree will be very small. Often only used as an intermediate stem piece on MM.106 or MM.111. If handled and spaced properly, it can be a very productive stock for a vertical axe system. Trees can be grown three to four feet tall and produce about 45 fruit, roughly 2 pecks, depending on fruit cultivar.

  M.9: Very dwarfing - Reaches a height of 8 to 10 ft (3 m), coming into fruit after 3-4 years, reaching full capacity of 50 to 65lb (20 kg) after 5 to 6 years. It will grow under average soil conditions, but needs a good rich soil to thrive. A good choice where space is limited and fertility is high. Permanent staking is required, as is routine feeding and watering. Trees on this rootstock always require leader support. The rootstock is very susceptible to fire blight and can develop burr knots.

- *G.41* Geneva 41, released in 2005, produces trees the size of M.9. The rootstock was developed from a cross between M.27 and Robusta 5 made in 1975. Resistant to Crown | Collar | Root rot(Phytopthora) and fire blight.
- *M.26:* Dwarfing - Similar to M9 in effect, although somewhat more vigorous and generally stronger, with a higher expected eventual yield of 65-75 lb (35 kg) and height of 8 to 10 ft (3 m). A good choice where soil quality is average and compact growth is required. Comes into fruit after 3-4 years, reaching full cropping capacity after 5 to 6 years. Staking needed for first five years of its life *citation needed*] It is susceptible to collar rot and fire blight and should not be planted in a wet site. Certain varieties when grafted onto this rootstock may exhibit signs of graft union incompatibility (i.e., the union breaks).
- *G.11* Geneva 11 is the second release of the Cornell breeding programme similar in size to M.26(Class 4) but more productive. Has the advantage of being resistant to fire blight and crown rot as well as only rarely producing suckers or burr knots.
- *G.202* Geneva 202(CG 5202) is a semidwarfing rootstock that produces a tree in class 5 slightly larger than M.26(Size Class 4) and is more productive than M.26. It was developed from a cross of M.27 (Size Class 1) and Robusta 5 to be fire blight and Phytopthora resistant as well as having resistance to woolly apple aphids. In a 9-year study with the scion cultivar of the "Liberty" apple, G.202 was about 50 percent smaller than M.7 but had much greater production efficiency.
- *M.7* Malling 7 rootstock produces a semidwarf tree of Class 6 that is freestanding in deep well drained soils but in rocky,

steep, or shallow soils, it tends to lean. The rootstock may sucker profusely and is susceptible to collar rot(Phytopthora).

- *MM.106:* Semi-dwarfing - Sometimes referred to as semi-vigorous, this is the most widely used of rootstocks. It is probably the best choice for the average garden under average conditions, being tolerant of a wide range of soils, and producing a tree with an eventual size of 14 to 18 ft (5 m). Trees on this stock begin producing fruit within three to four years, and yield up to 90 to 110 lb (50 kg) after some seven or eight years MM106 is very suitable for use with weaker varieties that would produce under sized bushes with more dwarfing rootstocks. Can be trained as a half standard tree, but is rather too vigorous for cordons unless the soil is poor. Requires staking for the first five years or so of its life Trees on MM.106 are highly susceptible to collar rot especially when planted in soils that remain wet.
- *M.111*: Vigorous - Not generally suitable for garden scale growing, being both too large and spreading (18-25'), and too slow to come into cropping. They are however suitable for growing as specimen standards in the large garden, or for producing medium sized bushes on poorer soils. Begins to fruit after six or seven years, reaching full capacity of 160 to 360 lb (80 to 180 kg) after eight to nine years It is the most cold-hardy rootstock readily available. Planting depth of this rootstock is critical. The union should be no higher than 1 to 2 inches above the final soil line.
- *M.25:* Very vigorous - Suitable for a grassed orchard, and to grow on as a full standard. Plant 20 ft (7 m) apart, makes a tree of 15 to 20 ft (5 m) or more height and spread, eventually yielding 200 to 400 lb (100 to 200 kg) per tree This rootstock is primarily used in UK and is rarely seen in USA where M.111 is used for this size tree.
- *Seedling:* Very vigorous trees produced on a rootstock grown from seed. There is greater variability than with the vegetatively propagated rootstocks. Apples used for

production of seedling rootstocks include 'Dolgo' and 'Antonovka', which are both extremely hardy and vigorous.

That is only a sample of some of the more important current apple rootstocks that are available. There are at least a hundred more that have been developed to either provide enhancement or prevent potential damage from one kind of pest or another.

The problem with growing fruit trees, especially apple trees, is that they are subject to many different types of damage from bacteria, fungi and insects. The general approach of the commercial industry has been to use as many chemicals as necessary to insure attractive and marketable fruit. The attitude, still prevalent, has been "Who cares? Nobody eats a tree!" but as environmental problems increase and the general public pushes for low or no-spray fruit, there has become a commercial need for fruit that does not require such intensive spray programmes. This is being achieved, albeit slowly, by rootstocks and trees that are bred to have natural disease and pest resistance.

The Malling series and clones have been standard rootstocks for apples for many years and remain the standard "workhorses" for the commercial industry (in USA). However, since most of them are susceptible to disease some Malling rootstocks are being replaced by new breeds, including the Cornell-Geneva series. One of the newest rootstocks, only released commercially in 2004, is CG5202(G.202) which adds resistance to the woolly apple aphid(WAA) for the "CG" series of stocks which already has resistance to the major problems preventing quality production of apples utilizing organic control systems. Combined with highly resistant trees such as "Liberty" it is showing great potential.

That leads to another characteristic of rootstocks that is or can be bred into them: environmental adaptability. This may be tolerance to wetdry soil conditions, acidity alkalinity of soil or even hot cold air temperature.

The ability of rootstocks to modify or augment characteristics of fruit trees is limited and often disappointing in the final results. It takes ten years to get a full picture of the effects of any one rootstock so a rootstock that appears promising in the first five years of a trial may fail in the last five years. The Mark (apple) rootstock was such a stock and has now fallen mostly into disfavor Another, the G.30, has proved to be an excellent stock for production but it was only after a number of years of trials that it was found to be somewhat incompatible with "Gala" apple (and possibly others) so that it is now recommended to be staked and wired.

To get a clear picture and push the industry forward, a consortium was founded and the so-called "NC-140" trials of rootstocks began. These test many pome rootstocks in many different sites across the USA and thereby provide growers, be they backyard or commercial, a clearer picture of what to expect when growing fruit trees on specific stock, in specific planting methods in their specific area of the USA. As one can imagine, this has the potential for a large economic benefit to both growers and consumers as well as going a long way to eliminating the need to spray pesticides as frequently as is currently required.

PEAR ROOTSTOCKS

Pears are usually grafted onto quince rootstocks, which produce small to medium sized trees. Some varieties however are not compatible with quince, and these require double working. This means that a piece of pear graft-work compatible with both the quince rootstock and the pear variety is used as an intermediate between the two. If this is not done the pear and the rootstock could eventually separate at the graft. Varieties that require double working include 'Bristol Cross', 'Dr Jules Guyot', 'Doyenné d' été' and 'Williams Bon Chrétien'.

- *Quince C:* Moderately vigorous- Makes a bush pear tree about 8 to 18 ft (3 to 6 m) tall, bearing fruit within four to eight years. Suitable for highly fertile soils and vigorous varieties, but not where conditions are poor. Used for bush, cordon and espalier growing. Old stocks of Quince C may be infected with a virus, so care should be taken to obtain certified virus free stock. If in doubt, use Quince A as there is not a great amount of difference in vigour between the two.

- *Quince A:* Medium vigour- Slightly more vigorous than Quince C, this is the most common variety upon which pears are grafted. Bears fruit between four to eight years, making a tree of some 10 to 20 ft (3 to 7 m) in height and spread. Suitable for all forms of pear trees except standards.

Pear stock: Very vigorous- Pears grafted onto pear rootstocks make very large standard trees, not suitable for most gardens.

Cherries

Until the 1970s, cherries were grown of the vigorous Malling F12/1, Mazzard (*Prunus avium*), or Maheleb (*P. maheleb*) rootstocks, which required much space and time before cropping began, thus the growing of cherries was not a realistic option on a garden scale. The introduction of the rootstock 'Colt' enables trees reaching a maximum height of 12 to 15 ft (4 to 5 m) to be grown, and if trained as a pyramid it is possible to restrict growth to about 10 ft (3 m). The popular sweet variety 'Stella' could even be grafted onto a 'Colt' rootstock and successfully grown in a pot on the patio.

Plums

Plum rootstocks include:

- *Pixy* - A dwarfing rootstock, suitable for bush trees planted 8-10 (3 m) apart.
- *St. Julien A* - A semi vigorous rootstock suitable for bush and half standards planted 12 to 15 ft (4 to 5 m) apart. Also suitable for peaches, nectarines and apricots.
- Brompton or Myrobalan B- Suitable for half standards planted 18 to 22 ft (6 to 7 m) apart. Also suitable for peaches, nectarines and apricots.
- *Myro-29C* - Semi-dwarf rootstock. Shallow, vigorous, good choice for hard soils. Somewhat drought tolerant.
- *Citation* - Semi-dwarf rootstock. Shallow, vigorous, good choice for hard soils. Prefers a wetter soil.

Some species of fruit are commonly grown on their own roots; new plants are propagated by rooting, layering, or modern tissue-culture techniques. In these cases there are may be no great advantages to using a special rootstock or improved rootstocks are not available.

Though vegetative propagation of apple, pear, stone fruits, and many other species is a nearly universal practice, it does have some detractors. Here is an account of one advocate of own-root fruit trees.

Own-root Apples in a Permaculture Design

Permaculture designer and fruit nurseryman Phil Corbett has for a number of years been working on an innovative project involving growing fruit trees on their own roots. His work is based on research carried out by Hugh Ermen of the Brogdale Horticultural Research Station, home of the National Apple Collection. Corbett writes; "Hugh discovered that there are several advantages in growing apples on their own roots- that is, not grafted onto a rootstock. The graft union, which is a union between two genetically different individuals, always creates a degree of incompatibility. Not having this incompatibility, own-root trees were found to have better health and better fruit quality. The only disadvantage of own-root trees is that most varieties are more vigorous than is usually wanted. This means that trees may make a lot of wood at the expense of fruit bud production, giving big trees that take a long time to come into crop. Conventionally this vigour is controlled by grafting onto a dwarfing rootstock. With trees on their own roots, however, a number of traditional techniques can induce early cropping. Once cropping begins, the tree's energies are channelled into fruit production and growth slows down to a controllable level. The techniques that are usually sufficient to bring about cropping are:

- Withholding nitrogen, which would stimulate growth, and withholding irrigation, except in serious drought;
- Tying down one and two year old branches to the horizontal. This induces fruit bud formation;

- Prune in summer to stimulate fruit buds to form, and avoid winter pruning which stimulates regrowth.

Once cropping has begun, a normal feeding and watering regime can begin. The average cropping own-root tree can be maintained at a size very similar to the same variety on MM106 rootstock" (Phil Corbett, from *The Common Ground Book of Orchards*, pub Common Ground, 2000).

He is also conducting research into the 'coppice-ability' of own-root fruit trees, including an experimental 'Coppice Orchard' project, wherein own-root trees are planted in north-south rows; "When the canopy of the orchard closes, a north-south row will be coppiced and the land in the row used for light demanding crops while the trees regrow. The trees on either side of the glade will have higher light levels on their sides and produce more fruit buds". Over time a series of parallel sheltered glades will be created which will be coppiced on a rotational basis, allowing for multifunctional use of land in order to produce not only fruit but also small wood products, soft fruit, vegetables and even possibly cereals, fungi and the more traditional bees and poultry. This is a project with much promising potential, and deserving of attention from the wider organic growing movement for the valuable lessons that will no doubt be provided over time.

Fruit Tree Pollination

Most Apples are self incompatible and must be cross pollinated. A few are described as "self-fertile" and are capable of self-pollination although they tend to carry larger crops when pollinated. A relatively small number of species are "Triploid", meaning that they provide no viable pollen for themselves or other apple trees. Apples that can pollinate one another are grouped by the time they usually flower so cross-pollinators are in bloom at the same time. Pollination management is an important component of apple culture. Before planting, it is important to arrange for pollenizers - varieties of apple or crabapple that provide plentiful, viable and compatible pollen. Orchard blocks may alternate rows of compatible varieties, or may plant crabapple trees, or graft on limbs of crabapple. Some varieties produce very little pollen, or the pollen is sterile, so these are not good pollenizers. Good-quality nurseries have pollenizer compatibility lists.

Growers with old orchard blocks of single varieties sometimes provide bouquets of crabapple blossoms in drums or pails in the orchard for pollenizers. Home growers with a single tree and no other variety in the neighborhood can do the same on a smaller scale.

During the bloom each season, apple growers usually provide pollinators to carry the pollen. Honeybee hives are most commonly used, and arrangements may be made with a commercial beekeeper who supplies hives for a fee.

Orchard mason bees are also used as supplemental pollinators in commercial orchards. Home growers may find these more acceptable in suburban locations because they do not sting. Some wild bees such as carpenter bees and other solitary bees may help. Bumble bee queens are sometimes present in orchards, but not usually in enough quantity to be significant pollinators.

Symptoms of inadequate pollination are small and misshapen apples, and slowness to ripen. The seeds can be counted to evaluate pollination. Well-pollinated apples are the best quality, and will have seven to ten seeds. Apples with fewer than three seeds will usually not mature and will drop from the trees in the early summer. Inadequate pollination can result from either a lack of pollinators or pollenizers, or from poor pollinating weather at bloom time. It generally requires multiple bee visits to deliver sufficient grains of pollen to accomplish complete pollination.

This is a list of Apple Tree Flowering Groups for the UK. You can use it as a reference for the purposes of ensuring you have the correct pollinator(s) available for your Apple trees. There are too many varieties for it to be inclusive, so please add as appropriate.

Early Flowering Group

These trees will pollinate one another and any tree in the Mid Season Flowering Group (see) below:

Beauty of Bath, Discovery, Egremont Russet

Mid Season Flowering Group

These trees will pollinate one another and any tree in either the Early or Late Season Flowering Groups:

Arthur Turner, Charles Ross, Cox's Orange Pippin, Cox's Self-Fertile, Grenadier, James Grieve, Lord Lambourne, Revd W. Wilkes, Sunset, Winter Gem, Worcester Permain.

Triploids in this group (that need pollination but cannot pollinate other trees) are:

Blenheim Orange, Bramley's Seedling

Late Season Flowering Group

These trees will pollinate one another and any tree in the Mid Season Flowering Group:

Ellisons Orange, Falstaff, Howgate Wonder, Laxton's Superb, Spartan

Triploids in this group (that need pollination but cannot pollinate other trees) are:

Crispin, Jupiter

Creative Commons Licence

Pear

Pears are similar to apples, with the notable exception that pear blossoms are much less attractive to bees, due to lower sugar content than apple or contemporaneous wildflower nectar. Bees may abandon the pear blossoms to visit dandelions or a nearby apple orchard. There are two possible methods used to compensate. One is saturation pollination, that is to stock so many bees that all area blossoms are worked regardless of the attractiveness to the bees. The other is to delay the movement of the beehives into the orchards until there is about 30 per cent bloom. The bees are moved into the orchard during the night and will usually visit the pear blossoms for a few hours until they discover the richer nectar sources. The recommended number of hives per acre is 1.

Citrus

Many citrus varieties are seedless and are produced parthenocarpically without pollination. Some varieties may be capable of producing fruit either way, having seeds in the segments, if pollinated, and no seeds if not.

Citrus that requires pollination may be self compatible, thus pollen must be moved only a short distance from the anther to the stigma by a pollinator. Some citrus, such as Meyer Lemons, are popular container plants. When these bloom indoors, they often suffer from blossom drop because no pollinators have access. Hand pollinate by a human pollinator is a solution, though it is important to learn whether the variety is self fertile or self incompatible.

A few citrus varieties, including some tangelos and tangerines are self incompatible, and require cross pollination. Pollenizers must be planned when groves are planted. This last group generally requires the addition of managed honeybee hives at bloom time for adequate pollination.

CHAPTER 7

Citrus Trees

SCIENTIFIC CLASSIFICATION

Kingdom	:	Plantae
(unranked)	:	Angiosperms
(unranked)	:	Eudicots
(unranked)	:	Rosids
Order	:	Sapindales
Family	:	Rutaceae
Subfamily	:	Aurantioideae
Tribe	:	Citreae
Genus	:	Citrus

Species and Hybrids

Important Species

- *Citrus aurantifolia* – Key Lime
- *Citrus maxima* – Pomelo
- *Citrus medica* – Citron
- *Citrus reticulata* – Mandarin Orange & Tangerine

Important Hybrids

- *Citrus × aurantium* – Bitter Orange
- *Citrus × latifolia* – Persian Lime
- *Citrus × limon* – Lemon
- *Citrus × limonia* – Rangpur
- *Citrus × paradisi* – Grapefruit
- *Citrus × sinensis* – Sweet Orange

Synonyms

Eremocitrus

Microcitrus

Citrus is a common term and genus of flowering plants in the family Rutaceae, originating in tropical and subtropical southeast regions of the world. The Latin word *citrus* was borrowed from ancient Greek *kedros* "cedar, juniper" probably through Etruscan. The Romans applied the word to several different trees with fragrant foliage or wood (compare the completely unrelated cedars). The taxonomy and systematics of the genus are complex and the precise number of natural species is unclear, as many of the named species are clonally-propagated hybrids, and there is genetic evidence that even some wild, true-breeding species are of hybrid origin Cultivated *Citrus* may be derived from as few as four ancestral species. Natural and cultivated origin hybrids include commercially important fruit such as the oranges, grapefruit, lemons, some limes, and some tangerines.

Recent research has suggested that the closely related genus *Fortunella* (kumquats), and perhaps also *Poncirus* and the Australian *Microcitrus* and *Eremocitrus*, should be included in *Citrus*. In fact, most botanists now classify *Microcitrus* and *Eremocitrus* as part of the genus *Citrus*.

SLICES OF VARIOUS CITRUS FRUITS

These plants are large shrubs or small trees, reaching 5-15 m tall, with spiny shoots and alternately arranged evergreen leaves with an entire margin. The flowers are solitary or in small corymbs, each flower 2–4 cm diameter, with five (rarely four) white petals and numerous stamens; they are often very strongly scented. The fruit is a *hesperidium*, a specialised berry, globose to elongated, 4–30 cm long and 4–20 cm diameter, with a leathery rind surrounding segments or "liths" filled with pulp vesicles. The genus is commercially important as many species are cultivated for their fruit, which is eaten fresh, pressed for juice, or preserved in marmalades.

Citrus fruits are notable for their fragrance, partly due to flavonoids and limonoids (which in turn are terpenes) contained in the rind, and most are juice-laden. The juice contains a high quantity of citric acid giving them their characteristic sharp flavour. They are also good sources of vitamin C and flavonoids.

PERSIAN LIMES IN A GROCERY STORE

Citrus trees hybridise very readily - depending on the pollen source, plants grown from a Persian Lime's seeds can produce fruit similar to grapefruit. Thus all commercial citrus cultivation uses trees produced by grafting the desired fruiting cultivars onto rootstocks selected for disease resistance and hardiness.

The colour of citrus fruits only develops in climates with a (diurnal) cool winter. In tropical regions with no winter, citrus fruits remain green until maturity, hence the tropical "green oranges". The Persian Lime in particular is extremely sensitive to cool conditions, thus it is usually never exposed to cool enough conditions to develop a mature colour. If they are left in a cool place over winter, the fruits will actually change to a yellow colour. Many citrus fruits are picked while still green, and ripened while in transit to supermarkets.

Citrus trees are not generally frost hardy. Mandarin Oranges (*C. reticulata*) tend to be the hardiest of the common *Citrus* species and can withstand short periods down to as cold as -10 °C, but realistically temperatures not falling below -2 °C are required for successful cultivation. Tangerines, tangors and yuzu can be grown outside even in regions with more marked sub-zero degrees in winter, although this may affect fruit quality.

A few hardy hybrids can withstand temperatures well below freezing, but do not produce quality fruit. Lemons can be commercially grown in cooler-summer/moderate-winter coastal Southern California, because sweetness is neither attained nor expected in retail lemon fruit. The related Trifoliate Orange (*Poncirus trifoliata*) can survive below -20 °C; its fruit are astringent and inedible unless cooked but a few better-tasting cultivars and hybrids have been developed.

The trees do best in a consistently sunny, humid environment with fertile soil and adequate rainfall or irrigation. Older 'abandoned' *Citrus* in low valleyland may suffer, yet survive, the dry summer of Central California's Inner Coast Ranges. At any age Citrus grows well enough with infrequent irrigation in partial/understory shade, but the fruit crop is smaller. Though broadleaved, they are evergreen and do not drop leaves except when stressed. The stems of many varieties have large sharp thorns. The trees flower in the spring, and fruit is set shortly afterward. Fruit begins to ripen in fall or early winter months, depending on cultivar, and develops increasing sweetness afterward. Some cultivars of tangerines ripen by winter. Some, such as the grapefruit, may take up to eighteen months to ripen.

Major commercial citrus growing areas include southern China, the Mediterranean Basin (including southern Spain), South Africa, Australia, the southernmost United States, and parts of South America. In the United States, Florida, California, Arizona, and Texas are major producers, while smaller plantings are present in other Sun Belt states.

Citrus trees grown in tubs and wintered under cover were a feature of Renaissance gardens, once glass-making technology enabled sufficient expanses of clear glass to be produced. An orangery was a feature of royal and aristocratic residences through the 17th and 18th centuries. The *Orangerie* at the Palace of the Louvre, 1617, inspired imitations that were not eclipsed until the development of the modern greenhouse in the 1840s. In the United States the earliest surviving orangery is at the Tayloe House, Mount Airy, Virginia. George Washington had an orangery at Mount Vernon.

Some modern hobbyists still grow dwarf citrus in containers or greenhouses in areas where it is too cold to grow it outdoors. Consistent climate, sufficient sunlight, and proper watering are crucial if the trees are to thrive and produce fruit. Compared to many of the usual "green shrubs", citrus trees better tolerate poor container care. For cooler winter areas, limes and lemons should not be grown, since they are more sensitive to winter cold than other citrus fruits. Hybrids with kumquats (× *Citrofortunella*) have good cold resistance.

LIST OF CITRUS DISEASES

Citrus plants are very liable to infestation by aphids, whitefly and scale insects (e.g. California red scale). Also rather important are the viral infections to which some of these ectoparasites serve as vectors such as the aphid-transmitted *Citrus tristeza virus* which when unchecked by proper methods of control is devastating to citrine plantations.

European brown snails (*Helix aspersa*) can be a problem in California, though laying female Khaki Campbell and other Mallard-based ducks can be used for control.

The foliage is also used as a food plant by the larvae of Lepidoptera (butterfly and moth) species such as the Geometridae *Hemithea aestivaria* (Common Emerald) and *Gymnoscelis rufifasciata* (Double-striped Pug), or the Arctiidae *Hypercompe scribonia* (Giant Leopard Moth), *H. eridanus*, *H. icasia* and *H. indecisa*.

Many citrus fruits, such as oranges, tangerines, grapefruits, and clementines, are generally eaten fresh. They are typically peeled and can be easily split into segments. Grapefruit is more commonly halved and eaten out of the skin with a spoon. There are special spoons (grapefruit spoons) with serrated tips designed for this purpose. Orange and grapefruit juices are also very popular breakfast beverages. More astringent citrus, such as lemons and limes are generally not eaten on their own. Meyer Lemons can be eaten 'out of hand' with the fragant skin; they are both sweet and sour. Lemonade or limeade are popular beverages prepared by diluting the juices of these fruits and adding sugar. Lemons and limes are also used as garnishes or in cooked dishes. Their juice is used as an ingredient in a variety of dishes; it can commonly be found in salad dressings and squeezed over cooked meat or vegetables. A variety of flavours can be derived from different parts and treatments of citrus fruits. The rind and oil of the fruit is generally very bitter, especially when cooked. The fruit pulp can vary from sweet and tart to extremely sour. Marmalade, a condiment derived from cooked orange and lemon, can be especially bitter. Lemon or lime is commonly used as a garnish for water, soft drinks, or cocktails. Citrus juices, rinds, or slices are used in a variety of mixed drinks. The colourful outer skin of some citrus fruits, known as zest, is used as a flavouring in cooking; the white inner portion of the peel, the pith, is usually avoided due to its bitterness. The zest of a citrus fruit, typically lemon or an orange, can also be soaked in water in a coffee filter, and drunk.

Medical

Citrus juice also has medical uses; lemon juice is used to relieve the pain of bee stings. The orange is also used in vitamin C pills, which prevents scurvy. Scurvy is caused by vitamin C deficiency, and can be prevented by having 10 milligrams of vitamin C a day. An early sign of scurvy is fatigue. If ignored, later symptoms are bleeding and bruising easily. After consumption, the peel is sometimes used as a facial cleanser. Before the development of fermentation-based processes, lemons were the primary commercial source of citric acid.

LIST OF CITRUS FRUITS

Citrons for sale in Germany.

Red Finger Lime, a rare delicacy from Australia.

Sweetie or Oroblanco.

Clementines have thinner skins than oranges.

Mikan, also known as satsumas.

Sweet oranges are used in many foods.

A batch of kaffir limes.

Lemons, whole and in sections.

The genus *Citrus* has been suggested to originate in Southeast Asia. Prior to human cultivation, it consisted of just a few species:

- Papedas
- *Citrus aurantifolia* – Key Lime, from India
- *Citrus halimii*, from Thailand and Malaya
- *Citrus maxima* – Pomelo (pummelo, shaddock), from the Malay Archipelago
- *Citrus medica* – Citron, from India
- *Citrus reticulata* – Mandarin oranges, from China
- Australian limes
- *Citrus australasica* – Finger Lime - sometimes separated in *Microcitrus*
- *Citrus australis* – Australian Round Lime - sometimes separated in *Microcitrus*
- *Citrus glauca* – Desert Lime - sometimes separated in *Eremocitrus* and 3 other *Microcitrus*

Kumquats are in the genus *Fortunella*.

Hybrids and Cultivars

Sorted by parentage. As each is the product of (at least) two parent species, they are listed multiple times.

- *Citrus maxima*-based
- Amanatsu, natsumikan – *Citrus* × *natsudaidai* (*C. maxima* × unknown)
- limequat
- Grapefruit, *Citrus* × *paradisi* (*C. maxima* × *C.* × *sinensis*)
- Imperial Lemon (*C.* × *limon* × *C.* × *paradisi*)
- Minneola Tangelo (*C. reticulata* × C. × paradisi)
- Orangelo, Chironja (*C.* × *paradisi* × *C.* × *sinensis*)
- Oroblanco, Sweetie (*C. maxima* × *C.* × *paradisi*)

- Sweet Orange – *Citrus* × *sinensis* (probably C. *maxima* × C. × *reticulata*)
- Tangelo – *Citrus* × *tangelo* (C. *reticulata* × C. maxima *or* C. × paradisi)
- Tangor – *Citrus* × *nobilis* (C. *reticulata* × C. × *sinensis*)
- Ugli (C. *reticulata* × C. *maxima* or C. × *paradisi*)
- Wilking (C. × *nobilis* × C. × *deliciosa*)
- *Citrus medica*-based
- Buddha's Hand – *Citrus medica* var. *sarcodactylus*
- Etrog
- Fernandina – *Citrus* × *limonimedica* (probably C. *medica* × C. × *limon*)
- Ponderosa Lemon (probably C. *medica* × C. × *limon*)
- *Citrus reticulata*-based
- Bergamot Orange, Seville Orange – *Citrus* × *aurantium* ssp. *bergamia* or *Citrus* × *bergamia*
- Bitter Orange – *Citrus* × *aurantium*
- Blood Orange – *Citrus* × *sinensis* · cultivars
- Cam sành (C. *reticulata* × C. × *sinensis*)
- Chinotto – *Citrus* × *aurantium* var. *myrtifolia* or *Citrus* × *myrtifolia*
- ChungGyun
- Clementine – *Citrus* × *clementina*
- Cleopatra Mandarin – *Citrus* × *reshni*
- Dekopon – *Citrus reticulata* cv. 'Siranui' (Kiyomi × Ponkan)
- Daidai – *Citrus* × *aurantium* var. *daidai* or *Citrus* × *daidai*
- Grapefruit, *Citrus* × *paradisi* (C. *maxima* × C. × *sinensis*)
- Hermandina
- Imperial Lemon (C. × *limon* × C. × *paradisi*)

- Kinnow
- Meyer Lemon, Valley Lemon – *Citrus* × *meyeri* (*C.* × *limon* × *C.* × *paradisi* or *C.* × *sinensis*)
- Michal Mandarin
- Mikan, satsuma – *Citrus* × *unshiu*
- Minneola Tangelo (*C. reticulata* × C. × paradisi)
- Nova Mandarin
- Orangelo, Chironja (*C.* × *paradisi* × *C.* × *sinensis*)
- Oroblanco, Sweetie (*C. maxima* × *C.* × *paradisi*)
- Ponkan
- Rangpur, Lemanderin, Mandarin Lime – *Citrus* × *limonia* (*C. reticulata* × *C.* × *limon*)
- Sweet Orange – *Citrus* × *sinensis* (probably *C. maxima* × C. × *reticulata*)
- Tangelo – *Citrus* × *tangelo* (*C. reticulata* × C. maxima *or* C. × paradisi)
- Tangerine
- Tangor – *Citrus* × *nobilis* (*C. reticulata* × *C.* × *sinensis*)
- Ugli (*C. reticulata* × C. maxima *or* C. × paradisi)
- Wilking (*C.* × *nobilis* × *C.* × *deliciosa*)
- Willow Leaf – · *Citrus* × *deliciosa*
- Yuzu – *Citrus* × *junos* (*C. reticulata* × *C.* × *ichangensis*)
- Unresolved
- Alemow, Colo – *Citrus* × *macrophylla*
- Djeruk limau – *Citrus* × *amblycarpa*
- Gajanimma, Carabao Lime – *Citrus* × *pennivesiculata*
- Ichang Lemon, Ichang papeda – *Citrus* × *ichangensis*
- Imperial Lemon (*C.* × *limon* × *C.* × *paradisi*)
- Iyokan, anadomikan

- Kabosu – *Citrus* × *sphaerocarpa*
- Kaffir Lime, makrut – *Citrus* × *hystrix*
- Khasi Papeda – *Citrus* × *latipes*
- Lemon – *Citrus* × *limon*
- Limetta, Sweet Lemon, Sweet Lime, mosambi – *Citrus* × *limetta*
- Omani Lime
- Palestine Sweet Lime – *Citrus* × *limettioides*
- Persian lime, Tahiti Lime – *Citrus* × *latifolia*
- Rough Lemon – *Citrus* × *jambhiri*
- Shekwasha, Hirami Lemon, Taiwan Tangerine – *Citrus* × *depressa*
- Sudachi – *Citrus* × *sudachi*
- Sunki, Suenkat – *Citrus* × *sunki*
- Tachibana Orange
- Volkamer Lemon – *Citrus* × *volkameriana*

CHAPTER 8

Importance of Wood

INTRODUCTION

Wood is hard, fibrous, lignified structural tissue produced as secondary xylem in the stems of woody plants, notably trees but also shrubs. In a living tree it conducts water and nutrients to the leaves and other growing tissues, and has a support function, enabling plants to reach large sizes. Wood may also refer to other plant materials and tissues with comparable properties.

People have used wood for millennia for many purposes, primarily as a construction material, for making tools, weapons, furniture, packaging, artworks, paper, and as a fuel. Wood can be dated by dendrochronology and carbon dating to make inferences about when a wooden object was created and the varying tree-ring widths and isotopic abundances give clues to the prevailing climate at that time.

A tree increases in diameter by the formation, between the old wood and the inner bark, of new woody layers which envelop the entire stem, living branches, and roots. Where there are clear seasons, this can happen in a discrete pattern, leading to what is known as growth rings, as can be seen on the end of a log. If these seasons are annual these growth rings are annual rings. Where there is no seasonal difference growth rings are likely to be indistinct or absent.

Within a growth ring it may be possible to see two parts. The part nearest the center of the tree is more open textured and almost invariably lighter in colour than that near the outer portion of the ring. The inner portion is formed early in the season, when growth is comparatively rapid; it is known as early wood or spring wood. The outer portion is the late wood or summer wood, being produced in the summer In white pines there is not much contrast in the different parts of the ring, and as a result the wood is very uniform in texture and is easy to work. In hard pines, on the other hand, the late wood is very dense and is deep-colored, presenting a very decided contrast to the soft, straw-colored early wood. In ring-porous woods each season's growth is always well defined, because the large pores of the spring abut on the denser tissue of the fall before. In the diffuse-porous woods, the demarcation between rings is not always so clear and in some cases is almost (if not entirely) invisible to the unaided eye.

KNOTS

A knot is a particular type of imperfection in a piece of timber, which reduces its strength, but which may be exploited for artistic effect. In a longitudinally-sawn plank, a knot will appear as a roughly circular "solid" (usually darker) piece of wood around which the roughly parallel fibres (grain) of the rest of the "flows" (parts and rejoins).

A knot is actually a portion of a side branch (or a dormant bud) included in the wood of the stem or larger branch. The included portion is irregularly conical in shape (hence the roughly circular cross-section) with the tip at the point in stem diameter at which the plant's cambium was located when the branch formed as a bud. Within a knot, the fibre direction (grain) is up to 90 degrees different from the fibres of the stem, thus producing local cross grain.

During the development of a tree, the lower limbs often die, but may persist for a time, sometimes years. Subsequent layers of growth of the attaching stem are no longer intimately joined with the dead limb, but are grown around it. Hence, dead branches produce knots which are not attached, and likely to drop out after the tree has been sawn into boards.

In grading lumber and structural timber, knots are classified according to their form, size, soundness, and the firmness with which they are held in place. This firmness is affected by, among other factors, the length of time for which the branch was dead while the attaching stem continued to grow.

Knots materially affect cracking (known in the industry as checking) and warping, ease in working, and cleavability of timber. They are defects which weaken timber and lower its value for structural purposes where strength is an important consideration. The weakening effect is much more serious when timber is subjected to forces perpendicular to the grain and/or tension than where under load along the grain and/or compression. The extent to which knots affect the strength of a beam depends upon their position, size, number, direction of fiber, and condition. A knot on the upper side is compressed, while one on the lower side is subjected to tension. If there is a season check in the knot, as is often the case, it will offer little resistance to this tensile stress. Small knots, however, may be located along the neutral plane of a beam and increase the strength by preventing longitudinal shearing. Knots in a board or plank are least injurious when they extend through it at right angles to its broadest surface. Knots which occur near the ends of a beam do not weaken it. Sound knots which occur in the central portion one-fourth the height of the beam from either edge are not serious defects.

Knots do not necessarily influence the stiffness of structural timber. Only defects of the most serious character affect the elastic limit of beams. Stiffness and elastic strength are more dependent upon the quality of the wood fiber than upon defects in the beam. The effect of knots is to reduce the difference between the fiber stress at elastic limit and the modulus of rupture of beams. The breaking strength is very susceptible to defects. Sound knots do not weaken wood when subject to compression parallel to the grain.

For purposes for which appearance is more important than strength, such as wall panelling, knots are considered a benefit, as they add visual texture to the wood, giving it a more interesting appearance.

The traditional style of playing the Basque xylophon *txalaparta* involves hitting the right knots to obtain different tones.

HEARTWOOD AND SAPWOOD

Heartwood is wood that has died and become resistant to decay as a result of genetically programmed processes. It appears in a cross-section as a discolored circle, following annual rings in shape. Heartwood is usually much darker than living wood, and forms with age. Many woody plants do not form heartwood, but other processes, such as decay, can discolor wood in similar ways, leading to confusion. Some uncertainty still exists as to whether heartwood is truly dead, as it can still chemically react to decay organisms, but only once.

Sapwood is living wood in the growing tree. All wood in a tree is first formed as sapwood. Its principal functions are to conduct water from the roots to the leaves and to store up and give back according to the season the food prepared in the leaves. The more leaves a tree bears and the more vigorous its growth, the larger the volume of sapwood required. Hence trees making rapid growth in the open have thicker sapwood for their size than trees of the same species growing in dense forests. Sometimes trees grown in the open may become of considerable size, 30 cm or more in diameter, before any heartwood begins to form, for example, in second-growth hickory, or open-grown pines.

The term *heartwood* derives solely from its position and not from any vital importance to the tree. This is evidenced by the fact that a tree can thrive with its heart completely decayed. Some species begin to form heartwood very early in life, so having only a thin layer of live sapwood, while in others the change comes slowly. Thin sapwood is characteristic of such trees as chestnut, black locust, mulberry, osage-orange, and sassafras, while in maple, ash, hickory, hackberry, beech, and pine, thick sapwood is the rule.

There is no definite relation between the annual rings of growth and the amount of sapwood. Within the same species the cross-sectional area of the sapwood is very roughly proportional to the size of the crown of the tree. If the rings are narrow, more of them are required than where they are wide. As the tree gets larger, the sapwood must necessarily become thinner or increase materially in volume. Sapwood is thicker in the upper portion of the trunk of a tree than near the base, because the age and the diameter of the upper sections are less.

When a tree is very young it is covered with limbs almost, if not entirely, to the ground, but as it grows older some or all of them will eventually die and are either broken off or fall off. Subsequent growth of wood may completely conceal the stubs which will however remain as knots. No matter how smooth and clear a log is on the outside, it is more or less knotty near the middle. Consequently the sapwood of an old tree, and particularly of a forest-grown tree, will be freer from knots than the heartwood. Since in most uses of wood, knots are defects that weaken the timber and interfere with its ease of working and other properties, it follows that sapwood, because of its position in the tree, may have certain advantages over heartwood.

It is remarkable that the inner heartwood of old trees remains as sound as it usually does, since in many cases it is hundreds of years, and in a few instances thousands of years, old. Every broken limb or root, or deep wound from fire, insects, or falling timber, may afford an entrance for decay, which, once started, may penetrate to all parts of the trunk. The larvae of many insects bore into the trees and their tunnels remain indefinitely as sources of weakness. Whatever advantages, however, that sapwood may have in this connection are due solely to its relative age and position.

If a tree grows all its life in the open and the conditions of soil and site remain unchanged, it will make its most rapid growth in youth, and gradually decline. The annual rings of growth are for many years quite wide, but later they become narrower and narrower. Since each succeeding ring is laid down on the outside of the wood previously formed, it follows that unless a tree materially increases its production of wood from year to year, the rings must necessarily become thinner as the trunk gets wider.

As a tree reaches maturity its crown becomes more open and the annual wood production is lessened, thereby reducing still more the width of the growth rings. In the case of forest-grown trees so much depends upon the competition of the trees in their struggle for light and nourishment that periods of rapid and slow growth may alternate. Some trees, such as southern oaks, maintain the same width of ring for hundreds of years. Upon the whole, however, as a tree gets larger in diameter the width of the growth rings decreases.

There may be decided differences in the grain of heartwood and sapwood cut from a large tree, particularly one that is mature. In some trees, the wood laid on late in the life of a tree is softer, lighter, weaker, and more even-textured than that produced earlier, but in other species, the reverse applies. In a large log the sapwood, because of the time in the life of the tree when it was grown, may be inferior in hardness, strength, and toughness to equally sound heartwood from the same log.

DIFFERENT WOODS

There is a strong relationship between the properties of wood and the properties of the particular tree that yielded it. For every tree species there is a range of density for the wood it yields. There is a rough correlation between density of a wood and its strength (mechanical properties). For example, while mahogany is a medium-dense hardwood which is excellent for fine furniture crafting, balsa is light, making it useful for model building. The densest wood may be black ironwood.

Wood is commonly classified as either softwood or hardwood. The wood from conifers (e.g. pine) is called softwood, and the wood from broad-leaved trees (e.g. oak) is called hardwood. These names are a bit misleading, as hardwoods are not necessarily hard, and softwoods are not necessarily soft. The well-known balsa (a hardwood) is actually softer than any commercial softwood. Conversely, some softwoods (e.g. yew) are harder than most hardwoods.

Wood products such as plywood are typically classified as engineered wood and not considered raw wood.

Colour

In species which show a distinct difference between heartwood and sapwood the natural colour of heartwood is usually darker than that of the sapwood, and very frequently the contrast is conspicuous. This is produced by deposits in the heartwood of various materials resulting from the process of growth, increased possibly by oxidation and other chemical changes, which usually have little or no appreciable effect on the mechanical properties of the wood. Some experiments on very resinous Longleaf Pine specimens, however, indicate an increase in strength. This is due to the resin which increases the strength when dry. Such resin-saturated heartwood is called "fat lighter". Structures built of fat lighter are almost impervious to rot and termites; however they are very flammable. Stumps of old longleaf pines are often dug, split into small pieces and sold as kindling for fires. Stumps thus dug may actually remain a century or more since being cut. Spruce impregnated with crude resin and dried is also greatly increased in strength thereby. The wood of Coast Redwood is distinctively red in colour.

Since the late wood of a growth ring is usually darker in colour than the early wood, this fact may be used in judging the density, and therefore the hardness and strength of the material. This is particularly the case with coniferous woods. In ring-porous woods the vessels of the early wood not infrequently appear on a finished surface as darker than the denser late wood, though on cross sections of heartwood the reverse is commonly true. Except in the manner just stated the colour of wood is no indication of strength.

Abnormal discolouration of wood often denotes a diseased condition, indicating unsoundness. The black check in western hemlock is the result of insect attacks. The reddish-brown streaks so common in hickory and certain other woods are mostly the result of injury by birds. The discolouration is merely an indication of an injury, and in all probability does not of itself affect the properties of the wood. Certain rot-producing fungi impart to wood characteristic colours which thus become symptomatic of weakness; however an attractive effect known as spalting produced by this process is often considered a desirable characteristic. Ordinary sap-staining is due to fungous growth, but does not necessarily produce a weakening effect.

STRUCTURE OF A WOOD

Wood is a heterogeneous, hygroscopic, cellular and anisotropic material. It is composed of fibers of cellulose (40%-50%) and hemicellulose (15%-25%) impregnated with lignin (15%-30%).

In coniferous or softwood species the wood cells are mostly of one kind, tracheids, and as a result the material is much more uniform in structure than that of most hardwoods. There are no vessels ("pores") in coniferous wood such as one sees so prominently in oak and ash, for example.

They are more or less filled with vessels: in some cases (oak, chestnut, ash) quite large and distinct, in others (buckeye, poplar, willow) too small to be seen plainly without a small hand lens. In discussing such woods it is customary to divide them into two large classes, *ring-porous* and *diffuse-porous*. In ring-porous species, such as ash, black locust, catalpa, chestnut, elm, hickory, mulberry, and oak, the larger vessels or pores (as cross sections of vessels are called) are localized in the part of the growth ring formed in spring, thus forming a region of more or less open and porous tissue. The rest of the ring, produced in summer, is made up of smaller vessels and a much greater proportion of wood fibres. These fibres are the elements which give strength and toughness to wood, while the vessels are a source of weakness.

In diffuse-porous woods the pores are scattered throughout the growth ring instead of being collected in a band or row. Examples of this kind of wood are basswood, birch, buckeye, maple, poplar, and willow. Some species, such as walnut and cherry, are on the border between the two classes, forming an intermediate group.

If a heavy piece of pine is compared with a light specimen it will be seen at once that the heavier one contains a larger proportion of late wood than the other, and is therefore considerably darker. The late wood of all species is denser than that formed early in the season, hence the greater the proportion of late wood the greater the density and strength. When examined under a microscope the cells of the late wood are seen to be very thick-walled and with very small cavities, while those formed first in the season have thin walls and large cavities. The strength is in the walls, not the cavities. In choosing a piece of pine where strength or stiffness is the important consideration, the principal thing to observe is the comparative amounts of early and late wood. The width of ring is not nearly so important as the proportion of the late wood in the ring.

It is not only the proportion of late wood, but also its quality, that counts. In specimens that show a very large proportion of late wood it may be noticeably more porous and weigh considerably less than the late wood in pieces that contain but little. One can judge comparative density, and therefore to some extent weight and strength, by visual inspection.

No satisfactory explanation can as yet be given for the real causes underlying the formation of early and late wood. Several factors may be involved. In conifers, at least, rate of growth alone does not determine the proportion of the two portions of the ring, for in some cases the wood of slow growth is very hard and heavy, while in others the opposite is true. The quality of the site where the tree grows undoubtedly affects the character of the wood formed, though it is not possible to formulate a rule governing it. In general, however, it may be said that where strength or ease of working is essential, woods of moderate to slow growth should be chosen. But in choosing a particular specimen it is not the width of ring, but the proportion and character of the late wood which should govern.

In the case of the ring-porous hardwoods there seems to exist a pretty definite relation between the rate of growth of timber and its properties. This may be briefly summed up in the general statement that the more rapid the growth or the wider the rings of growth, the heavier, harder, stronger, and stiffer the wood. This, it must be remembered, applies only to ring-porous woods such as oak, ash, hickory, and others of the same group, and is, of course, subject to some exceptions and limitations.

In ring-porous woods of good growth it is usually the middle portion of the ring in which the thick-walled, strength-giving fibers are most abundant. As the breadth of ring diminishes, this middle portion is reduced so that very slow growth produces comparatively light, porous wood composed of thin-walled vessels and wood parenchyma. In good oak these large vessels of the early wood occupy from 6 to 10 per cent of the volume of the log, while in inferior material they may make up 25 per cent or more. The late wood of good oak, except for radial grayish patches of small pores, is dark colored and firm, and consists of thick-walled fibers which form one-half or more of the wood. In inferior oak, such fiber areas are much reduced both in quantity and quality. Such variation is very largely the result of rate of growth.

Wide-ringed wood is often called "second-growth", because the growth of the young timber in open stands after the old trees have been removed is more rapid than in trees in the forest, and in the manufacture of articles where strength is an important consideration such "second-growth" hardwood material is preferred. This is particularly the case in the choice of hickory for handles and spokes. Here not only strength, but toughness and resilience are important. The results of a series of tests on hickory by the U.S. Forest Service show that:

> "The work or shock-resisting ability is greatest in wide-ringed wood that has from 5 to 14 rings per inch (rings 1.8-5 mm thick), is fairly constant from 14 to 38 rings per inch (rings 0.7-1.8 mm thick), and decreases rapidly from 38 to 47 rings per inch (rings 0.5-0.7 mm thick). The strength at maximum load is not so great with the most rapid-growing wood; it is maximum with from 14 to 20 rings per inch (rings 1.3-1.8 mm thick), and again becomes less as the wood becomes more closely ringed. The natural deduction is that wood of first-class mechanical value shows from 5 to 20 rings per inch (rings 1.3-5 mm thick) and that slower growth yields poorer stock. Thus the inspector or buyer of hickory should discriminate against timber that has more than 20 rings per inch (rings less than 1.3 mm thick). Exceptions exist, however, in the case of normal growth upon dry situations, in which the slow-growing material may be strong and tough."

The effect of rate of growth on the qualities of chestnut wood is summarized by the same authority as follows:

> "When the rings are wide, the transition from spring wood to summer wood is gradual, while in the narrow rings the spring wood passes into summer wood abruptly. The width of the spring wood changes but little with the width of the annual ring, so that the narrowing or broadening of the annual ring is always at the expense of the summer wood. The narrow vessels of the summer wood make it richer in wood substance than the spring wood composed of wide vessels. Therefore, rapid-growing specimens with wide rings have more wood substance than slow-growing trees with narrow rings. Since the more the wood substance the greater the weight, and the greater the weight the stronger the wood, chestnuts with wide rings must have stronger wood than chestnuts with narrow rings. This agrees with the accepted view that sprouts (which always have wide rings) yield better and stronger wood than seedling chestnuts, which grow more slowly in diameter."

In diffuse-porous woods, as has been stated, the vessels or pores are scattered throughout the ring instead of collected in the early wood. The effect of rate of growth is, therefore, not the same as in the ring-porous woods, approaching more nearly the conditions in the conifers. In general it may be stated that such woods of medium growth afford stronger material than when very rapidly or very slowly grown. In many uses of wood, strength is not the main consideration. If ease of working is prized, wood should be chosen with regard to its uniformity of texture and straightness of grain, which will in most cases occur when there is little contrast between the late wood of one season's growth and the early wood of the next.

MONOCOT WOOD

Structural tissue resembling ordinary 'dicot' wood is produced by a number of monocot plants, and these are also usually called wood. Of these, the wood of the grass bamboo has considerable economic importance, larger culms being used in the manufacture of engineered flooring, panels and veneer. Other plant groups that produce woody tissue are palms, and members of the Liliales, such as Dracaena and Cordyline. With all these woods, the structure and composition of the structural tissue is quite different from ordinary wood.

Water Content

The churches of Kizhi, Russia are among a handful of World Heritage Sites built entirely of wood, without metal joints.

Water occurs in living wood in three conditions, namely: (1) in the cell walls; (2) in the protoplasmic contents of the cells; and (3) as free water in the cell cavities and spaces. In heartwood it occurs only in the first and last forms. Wood that is thoroughly air-dried retains from 8-16% of water in the cell walls, and none, or practically none, in the other forms. Even oven-dried wood retains a small percentage of moisture, but for all except chemical purposes, may be considered absolutely dry.

The general effect of the water content upon the wood substance is to render it softer and more pliable. A similar effect of common observation is in the softening action of water on paper or cloth. Within certain limits, the greater the water content, the greater its softening effect.

Drying produces a decided increase in the strength of wood, particularly in small specimens. An extreme example is the case of a completely dry spruce block 5 cm in section, which will sustain a permanent load four times as great as that which a green block of the same size will support.

The greatest increase due to drying is in the ultimate crushing strength, and strength at elastic limit in endwise compression; these are followed by the modulus of rupture, and stress at elastic limit in cross-bending, while the modulus of elasticity is least affected.

Uses

Fuel

Wood is burned as a fuel mostly in rural areas of the world. Hard wood is preferred over softwood because it creates less smoke and burns longer. Adding a woodstove or fireplace to a home adds ambiance and warmth.

Construction

Wood can be cut into straight planks and made into a hardwood floor (parquetry).

Wood has been an important construction material since humans began building shelters, houses and boats. Nearly all boats were made out of wood till the late 19th century, and wood remains in common use today in boat construction. New domestic housing in many parts of the world today is commonly made from timber-framed construction. In buildings made of other materials, wood will still be found as a supporting material, especially in roof construction, in interior doors and their frames, and as exterior cladding. Wood to be used for construction work is commonly known as *lumber* in North America. Elsewhere, *lumber* usually refers to felled trees, and the word for sawn planks ready for use is *timber*. Wood is also commonly used as shuttering material to form the mould into which concrete is poured during reinforced concrete construction.

Wood unsuitable for construction in its native form may be broken down mechanically (into fibres or chips) or chemically (into cellulose) and used as a raw material for other building materials such as chipboard, engineered wood, hardboard, medium-density fiberboard (MDF), oriented strand board (OSB). Such wood derivatives are widely used: wood fibers are an important component of most paper, and cellulose is used as a component of some synthetic materials. Wood derivatives can also be used for kinds of flooring, for example laminate flooring.

Wood is also used for cutlery, such as chopsticks, toothpicks, and other utensils, like the wooden spoon.

In the Arts

Artists can use wood to create delicate sculptures.

Wood has long been used as an artistic medium. It has been used to make sculptures and carvings for centuries. Examples include the totem poles carved by North American indigenous people from conifer trunks, often Western Red Cedar (*Thuja plicata*), and the Millenium clock tower [9], now housed in the National Museum of Scotland[10] in Edinburgh.

It is also used in woodcut printmaking, and for engraving.

Certain types of musical instruments, such as those of the violin family, the guitar, the clarinet and recorder, the xylophone, and the marimba, are made mostly or entirely of wood. The choice of wood may make a significant difference to the tone and resonant qualities of the instrument, and tonewoods have widely differing properties, ranging from the hard and dense (african blackwood used for the bodies of clarinets to the light but resonant european spruce (*Picea abies*)) traditionally used for the soundboards of violins. The most valuable tonewoods, such as the ripple sycamore (*Acer pseudoplatanus*), used for the backs of violins, combine acoustic properties with decorative colour and grain which enhance the appearance of the finished instrument.

LIST OF WOODS

This is a list of woods, in particular those commonly used in the timber and lumber trade.

Softwoods (Conifers)

- Araucaria
- Hoop Pine (Aus.) *Araucaria cunninghamii*
- Parana Pine (Brazil) *Araucaria angustifolia*
- Pehuén or Chile Pine *Araucaria araucana*
- Cedar (*Cedrus*); also applied to a number of woods from trees in the Cypress family mainly in North America, see Redcedar, Whitecedar and Yellow-Cedar in Softwoods, and to woods from some relatives of the mahogany, see Spanish-cedar and Redcedar in Hardwoods.
- Cypress (*Chamaecyparis, Cupressus, Taxodium*)
- Arizona Cypress (*Cupressus arizonica*)
- Bald Cypress or Southern cypress (*Taxodium distichum*)

- Hinoki Cypress (*Chamaecyparis obtusa*)
- Lawson's Cypress (*Chamaecyparis lawsoniana*)
- Mediterranean Cypress (*Cupressus sempervirens*)
- Rocky Mountain Douglas-fir (*Pseudotsuga menziesii* var. *glauca*)
- European Yew (*Taxus baccata*)
- Fir (*Abies*)
- Balsam Fir (*Abies balsamea*)
- Silver Fir (*Abies alba*)
- Noble Fir (*Abies procera*)
- Pacific Silver Fir (*Abies amabilis*)
- Hemlock (*Tsuga*)
- Eastern Hemlock (*Tsuga canadensis*)
- Mountain Hemlock (*Tsuga mertensiana*)
- Western Hemlock (*Tsuga heterophylla*)
- Kauri (New Zealand) (*Agathis australis*)
- Kaya (*Torreya nucifera*)
- Larch (*Larix*)
- European Larch (*Larix decidua*)
- Japanese Larch (*Larix kaempferi*)
- Tamarack Larch or Tamarack (*Larix laricina*)
- Western Larch (*Larix occidentalis*)
- Pine (*Pinus;* Many woods are incorrectly called "Pine" See Araucaria and Douglas-fir above)
- Corsican pine (*Pinus nigra*)
- Jack Pine (*Pinus banksiana*)
- Lodgepole Pine (*Pinus contorta* subsp *latifolia*)
- Monterey Pine (*Pinus radiata*)

- Ponderosa Pine (*Pinus ponderosa*)
- Red Pine (N.Am.) (*Pinus resinosa*)
- Scots Pine, Red pine (UK), Red deal (UK), Redwood (UK, obsolete) (*Pinus sylvestris*)
- White Pine in (N.Am.), Yellow or Weymouth pine (UK, obsolete)
- Eastern White Pine (*Pinus strobus*)
- Western White Pine (*Pinus monticola*)
- Sugar Pine (*Pinus lambertiana*)
- Southern Yellow pine (US)
- Loblolly Pine (*Pinus taeda*)
- Longleaf Pine (*Pinus palustris*)
- Pitch Pine (*Pinus rigida*)
- Shortleaf Pine (*Pinus echinata*)
- "Redcedar"
- Eastern Redcedar, (*Juniperus virginiana*)
- Western redcedar (*Thuja plicata*)
- Redwood (*Sequoia sempervirens*)
- Rimu (New Zealand) (*Dacrydium cupressinum*)
- Spruce (*Picea*)
- Norway Spruce (*Picea abies*)
- Black Spruce (*Picea mariana*)
- Red Spruce (*Picea rubens*)
- Sitka Spruce (*Picea sitchensis*)
- White Spruce (*Picea glauca*)
- Sugi (*Cryptomeria japonica*)
- "Whitecedar"
- Northern Whitecedar (*Thuja occidentalis*)

- Southern Whitecedar (*Chamaecyparis thyoides*)
- "Yellow-cedar" (Nootka Cypress *Callitropsis nootkatensis,* formerly *Chamaecyparis nootkatensis*)

Hardwoods (Angiosperms)

- Afzelia (*Afzelia*)
- Agba yun (*Synsepalum duloificum*)
- Albizia (*Albizia*)
- Alder (*Alnus*)
- Black alder (*Alnus glutinosa*)
- Red alder (*Alnus rubra*)
- Applewood or wild apple (*Malus*)
- Ash (*Fraxinus*)
- Black ash (*Fraxinus nigra*)
- Blue ash (*Fraxinus quadrangulata*)
- Common ash (*Fraxinus excelsior*)
- Green ash (*Fraxinus pennsylvanica lanceolata*)
- Oregon ash (*F. latifolia*)
- Pumpkin ash (*F. profunda*)
- White ash (*Fraxinus americana*)
- Aspen (*Populus*)
- Bigtooth aspen (*Populus grandidentata*)
- European aspen (*Populus tremula*)
- Quaking aspen (*Populus tremuloides*)
- Ayan (*Distemonanthus benthamianus*)
- Balsa (*Ochroma pyramidale*)
- Basswood
- American basswood (*Tilia americana*)
- White basswood (*T. heterophylla*)

- Beech (*Fagus*)
- European Beech (*Fagus sylvatica*)
- American Beech (*Fagus grandifolia*)
- Birch (*Betula*)
- American birches
- Gray birch (*Betula populifolia*)
- River birch (*B. nigra*)
- Paper birch (*Betula papyrifera*)
- Sweet birch (*Betula lenta*)
- Yellow birch (*B. alleghaniensis* syn *Betula lutea*) - most common birch wood sold in N.Am.
- European birches, also Baltic birch (N.Am.)
- Silver birch (*Betula pendula*)
- White Birch (*Betula pubescens*)
- Blackbean (*Castanospermum australe*)
- Blackwood
- Australian Blackwood also Tasmanian Blackwood (*Acacia melanoxylon*)
- African Blackwood or Mpingo (*Dalbergia melanoxylon*)
- Bocote (*Cordia alliodora*)
- Boxelder (*Acer negundo*)
- Boxwood or Box (*Buxus sempervirens*)
- Brazilwood (*Caesalpinia echinata*)
- Bubinga (*Guibourtia*)
- Buckeye (*Aesculus*)
- Common Horse-chestnut (*Aesculus hippocastanum*)
- Ohio buckeye (*Aesculus glabra*)
- Yellow Buckeye (*Aesculus flava* syn. *Aesculus octandra*)

- Butternut (*Juglans cinerea*)
- Carapa (or Andiroba, Carap, Crappo, Crabwood and Santa Maria) (*Carapa guianensis*)
- Catalpa (*Catalpa*)
- Cherry (*Prunus*)
- Black cherry (*Prunus serotina*)
- Red cherry (*Prunus pennsylvanica*)
- Wild cherry (*Prunus avium*)
- "Brazilian Cherry" Not a Cherry
- Chestnut (*Castanea dentata*)
- Cape Chestnut (*Calodendrum capense*)
- Coachwood (*Ceratopetalum apetalum*)
- Cocobolo (*Dalbergia retusa*)
- Corkwood (*Leitneria floridana*)
- Cottonwood
- Balsam poplar (*Populus balsamifera*)
- Eastern cottonwood (*Populus deltoides*)
- Plains cottonwood (*Populus sargentii*)
- Swamp cottonwood (*Populus heterophylla*)
- Cucumbertree (*Magnolia acuminata*)
- Dogwood (*Cornus* spp.)
- Flowering dogwood (*Cornus florida*)
- Pacific dogwood (*Cornus nuttallii*)
- Ebony (*Diospyros*)
- Andaman marble-wood (India) (*Diospyros kurzii*)
- Ebène marbre (Mauritius, E. Africa) (*Diospyros melanida*)
- Gabon ebony, Black ebony, African ebony (*Diospyros crassiflora*)

- Elm
- American elm (*Ulmus americana*)
- English elm (*Ulmus procera*)
- Rock elm (*Ulmus thomasii*)
- Slippery elm (*Ulmus rubra*)
- Wych elm (*Ulmus glabra*)
- Eucalyptus (*Eucalyptus*)
- Lyptus
- Karri (W. Australia) (*Eucalyptus diversicolor*)
- Mahogany eucalyptus, (New South Wales) (*Eucalyptus*)
- Ironbark *Eucalyptus sideroxylon*
- Jarrah or West Australian eucalyptus (*Eucalyptus marginata*)
- Tasmanian oak or Mountain ash, (*Eucalyptus regnans Eucalyptus obliqua Eucalyptus delegatensis*)
- *River Red Gum*
- Blue Gum *Eucalyptus saligna*
- Greenheart (Guyana) (*Chlorocardium rodiei*)
- Grenadilla (Mpingo) (*Dalbergia melanoxylon*)
- Gum
- Blackgum (*Nyssa sylvatica*)
- Blue gum (*Eucalyptus globulus*)
- Redgum or Sweetgum (*Liquidambar styraciflua*)
- Tupelo gum (*Nyssa aquatica*)
- Hickory (*Carya*)
- Mockernut hickory (*Carya alba*)
- Pignut hickory (*Carya glabra*)
- Shagbark hickory (*Carya ovata*)
- Shellbark hickory (*Carya laciniosa*)

- Hornbeam (*Carpinus* species)
- Hophornbeam, Eastern (*Ostrya virginiana*)
- Ipê or Poui (*Tabebuia*)
- Iroko (*Milicia excelsa* syn *Chlorophora excelsa*)
- Ironwood refers to the wood of many tree species noted for the hardness of their wood. Trees commonly known as ironwoods include:
- *Carpinus caroliniana* — also known as American hornbeam
- *Casuarina equisetifolia* — Common Ironwood from Australia
- *Choricbangarpia subargentea*
- *Copaifera* spp.
- *Eusideroxylon zwageri*
- *Guajacum officinale* and *Guajacum sanctum* — Lignum vitae
- *Hopea odorata*
- "Ipe High in silica this wood makes a great decking material. Other common name " Brazilian Walnut"
- *Krugiodendron ferreum* — Black Ironwood
- *Lyonothamnus lyonii (L. floribundus)* — Catalina Ironwood
- *Mesua ferrea* — also known as Rose Chestnut or Ceylon Ironwood, from Thailand, Laos, Vietnam, Cambodia
- *Olea spp.* — various olive trees
- *Olneya tesota* — Desert Ironwood
- *Ostrya virginiana* — Hop hornbeam
- *Parrotia persica* — Persian Ironwood
- *Tabebuia serratifolia* — Yellow Lapacho
- Jacarandá, Brazilian rosewood (*Dalbergia nigra*)
- Jatobá (*Hymenaea courbaril*)
- Lacewood from the Sycamore (N.Am.) or Plane (UK) trees (*Platanus* species)

- Laurel, California (*Umbellularia californica*)
- Limba (*Terminalia superba*)
- Lignum vitae (*Guaiacum officinale* and *Guaiacum sanctum*)
- Locust
- Black locust or Yellow locust (*Robinia pseudacacia*)
- Honey locust (*Gleditsia triacanthos*)
- Mahogany
- Maple (*Acer*)
- Hard Maple (N.Am.)
- Sugar maple (*Acer saccharum*)
- Black maple (*Acer nigrum*)
- Soft Maple (N.Am.)
- Manitoba maple (*Acer negundo*)
- Red maple (*Acer rubrum*)
- Silver maple (*Acer saccharinum*)
- European Maples
- Sycamore maple (*Acer pseudoplatanus*)
- Meranti (*Shorea* sp.)
- Mpingo (Grenadilla) (*Dalbergia melanoxylon*)
- Oak (*Quercus*)
- American White Oak includes wood from any of the following species of trees.
- Bur oak (*Quercus macrocarpa*)
- White oak (*Quercus alba*)
- Post oak (*Quercus stellata*)
- Swamp white oak (*Quercus bicolor*)
- Southern live oak (*Quercus virginiana*)
- Swamp chestnut oak (*Quercus michauxii*)

- Chestnut oak (*Quercus prinus* or *Q. Montana*)
- Chinkapin oak (*Quercus muhlenbergii*)
- Canyon live oak (*Quercus chrysolepis*)
- Overcup oak (*Quercus lyrata*)
- English oak, also *French* and *Slovenian oak* barrels (*Quercus robur* and sometimes *Quercus petraea*)
- Red oak includes wood from any of the following species of trees:
- Red oak (*Quercus rubra*)
- Black oak (*Quercus velutina*)
- Laurel oak (*Quercus laurifolia*))
- Southern red oak (*Quercus falcata*)
- Water oak (*Quercus nigra*)
- Willow oak {*Quercus phellos*)
- Nuttall's oak (*Quercus texana* or *Q. nuttallii*)
- Willow oak (*Quercus phellos*)
- "Tasmanian oak"; Not an oak
- Australian "Silky oak"; Not an oak
- Obeche or Samba, Ayous, Arere, Wana, Abache (West Africa) (*Triplochiton scleroxylon*)
- Okoumé or "Gaboon" (*Aucoumea klaineana*)
- Oregon Myrtle or California Bay Laurel (*Umbellularia californica*)
- Pear (*Pyrus communis*)
- Pernambuco is another name for Brazilwood (*Caesalpinia echinata*)
- Poplar (*Populus*; in N.Am., wood sold as poplar is usually Yellow-poplar — see below)
- Balsam poplar (*Populus balsamifera*)

- Black poplar (*Populus nigra*)
- Hybrid poplar (*Populus* × *canadensis*)
- Ramin
- Redcedar (*Toona ciliata*)
- Rosewood (*Dalbergia* spp.)
- Sal (*Shorea robusta*)
- Sandalwood (*Santalum*)
- Sassafras (*Sassafras albidum*)
- Sassafras (Australia) (*Atherosperma moschatum*)
- Satinwood (Ceylon) (*Chloroxylon swietenia*)
- Silky Oak (*Grevillea robusta*) - Sold as Lacewood in North America
- Silver Wattle *Acacia dealbata*
- Snakewood
- Sourwood (*Oxydendrum arboreum*)
- Spanish-cedar (*Cedrela odorata*)
- American sycamore (*Platanus occidentalis*)
- Teak (*Tectona grandis*)
- Walnut (*Juglans*)
- Black Walnut (*Juglans nigra*)
- Persian Walnut (*Juglans regia*)
- Brazilian walnut; Not a walnut see Ipe above.
- Willow (*Salix*)
- Black willow (*Salix nigra*)
- Cricket-bat willow (*Salix alba* 'Coerulea')
- White willow (*Salix alba*)
- Yellow-poplar (*Liriodendron tulipifera*)

Hardwoods (monocotyledons)

- Bamboo (a number of species in Tribe: Bambuseae)
- Palmwood (*Cocos nucifera*) is 'new' wood source that is increasingly being used as an ecologically-sound alternative to endangered hardwoods.

WOOD ECONOMY

The existence of a wood economy, or more correctly, a forest economy (since in many countries a bamboo economy predominates), is a prominent matter in many developing countries as well as in many other nations with temperate climate and especially in those with low temperatures. These are generally the countries with greater forested areas. The uses of wood in furniture, buildings, bridges, and as a source of energy are widely known. Additionally, wood from trees and bushes, can be employed in a wide variety, including those produced from wood pulp, as cellulose in paper, celluloid in early photographic film, cellophane, and rayon (a substitute for silk).

At the end of their normal useage, wood products can be burnt to obtain thermal energy, or can be used as a fertilizer. The potential environmental damage that a wood economy could occasion include (problems of reduction the biodiversity due to monoculture forestry - the intensive cultivation of very few types of trees); and CO_2 emissions. However, forests can aid in reduction of atmospheric carbon dioxide and therefore diminish global warming.

The wood economy is historically the starting point of the civilizations worldwide, since eras preceding the Paleolithic and the Neolithic. It necessarily preceded [Bronze age | ages of metals]] by many centuries, as the melting of metals was possible only through the discovery of techniques to light fire (usually obtained by the scraping of two very dry wooden rods) and the building of many simple machines and rudimentary tools, as canes, club handles, bows, arrows, lances. One of the most ancient handmade articles ever found is one smoothed pricked of wood (Clacton Spear) 250,000 years old (third interglacial period), that was buried under sediments in England, at Clacton-on-Sea, and it was probably manifactured by the human-like species Homo erectus.

Successive civilizations such as the Egyptians and Sumerians built sophisticated objects of furniture. Many types of furniture in ivory and valuable woods have survived to our time practically intact, because secluded in inviolated secret tombs, they were protected from decay also by the dry environment of desert. Many buildings and parts of these (above all roofs) contained elements in wood (often of oak) forming structural supports and covering; means of transport such as boats, ships; and later (with the invention of the wheel) wagons and carriages, winches, flour mills powered by water, etc.

The main source of the lumber used in the world are forests, which can be classified in virgin, semivirgin and plantation. It is known that much timber is removed for firewood by the local populations in many countries, especially in third world, but this amount can only estimated, with wide margins of uncertainty.

In 1998, the world-wide production of wood, officially that not used as firewood (known as "roundwood"), was about 1.5 billions of cubic meters (m^3), amounting to around 45% of the wood cultivated in the world. Cut logs and branches destined to become elements for the construction of buildings account for approximately 55% of the World's industrial wood production. 25% becomes wood pulp (including wood powder and truccioli) mainly destined for the production of paper and cardboard; a further 20% approximately became panels in plywood and valuable wood for furnitures and objects of common use (FAO 1998) . The World's largest producer and consumer of this wood "officially accounted" is the USA, although the the country that possesses the greatest area of forests is Russia.

In the seventies, the countries with the biggest forest surface were: Soviet Union (approximately 8,800,000 km^2), Brazil (5,150,000 km^2), Canada (4,400,000 km^2), USA (3,000,000 km^2), Indonesia (1,200,000 km^2) and Democratic Republic of Congo (1,000,000 km^2). Other countries with important production and consumption of wood usually have a low density of population in relation to their territorial extension, here we can include countries as Argentina, Chile, Finland, Poland, Sweden, Ukraine.

By 2001 the rainforest areas of Brazil were reduced by a fifth (respect of 1970), to around 4,000,000 km^2; the ground cleared was mainly destined for cattle pasture - Brazil is the world's largest exporter of beef with almost 200,000,000 head of cattle. Also the booming ethanol economy that in Brazil is based upon sugar cane cultivation, is reducing forests size. Canadian forest was reduced to by almost 30% to 3,101,340 km^2 over the same period.

Importance in Fighting Greenhouse Effect

Regarding the problem of climate change, it is known that burning forests increase CO_2 in atmosphere, while intact virgin forest or plantations act as sinks for CO_2, for these reasons wood economy fights greenhouse effect. The amount of CO_2 absorbed depends on the type of trees, lands and the climate of the place where trees naturally grow or are planted. Moreover, should be told that by night plants do not execute photosynthesis, and produce CO_2, eliminated the successive day. Paradoxically in summer oxygen created by photosynthesis in forests near to cities and urban parks, interacts with urban air pollution (from cars, etc.) and is transformed by solar beams in ozone (molecule of three oxygen atoms), that while in high atmosphere constitutes a filter against ultraviolet beams, in the low atmosphere is a pollutant, able to provoke respiratory disturbances.

In a low-carbon economy, forestry operations will be focused on low-impact practices and regrowth. Forest managers will make sure that they do not disturb soil based carbon reserves too much. Specialized tree farms will be the main source of material for many products. Quick maturing tree varieties will be grown on short rotations in order to maximize output.

WOOD ECONOMY PER NATION/CONTINENTAL AREA

Australia

- *Eucalyptus:* these are seven hundred tree species from Australia, that grow very fast in tropical, sub-tropical and semi-arid climates, and are very resistant to forest fires (with their tree cortex) and to drought. Its essential oil is used in pharmacology, its wood for building, and the small branches as firewood and for paper and cardboard pulp.

Brazil

Brazil has a long tradition in the harvesting of several types of trees with specific uses. Since the sixties imported species of pine tree and eucalyptus have been grown mostly for the industry of paper pulp and plywood. Currently high-level research is being conducted, to apply the enzymes of sugar cane fermentation to cellulose in wood, in order to obtain methanol, but the cost is much higher compared ethanol derived from corn.

- *Brazilwood:* has a dense, orange-red heartwood that takes a high red shine (brasa=ember), and it is the premier wood used for making bows for string instruments from the violin family. This trees soon became the biggest source of red dye, and they were such a large part of the economy and export of that country, that slowly it was known as Brazil.
- *Hevea brasiliensis:* is the biggest source of the best latex, that is used to manufacture many objects in rubber, as an example gloves, condoms, anti-allergic mattresses and tires (vulcanized rubber). Latex has the ability to adjust to the exact shape of the body part, an advantage over polyurethane or polyethylene gloves.

Canada and USA

There is a close relation in the forestry economy between these countries, they have many tree genus in common, and Canada is the main producer of wood and wooden items destined to the USA, the biggest consumer of wood and it's byproducts in the world. The water systems of the Great Lakes, Erie canal, Hudson river and Saint Lawrence Seaway to the east coast and Mississippi to central plains and Louisiana allows transportation of logs at very low costs.

Canada

The agency Canada Wood Council calculates that by the year 1999 in Canada, the forest sector employed 850,000 workers

(1 job every 17), making around $74 billion of value in goods and services. For many years products derived from trees in Canadian forests had been the most important export items of the country. In 2001, exports around the world totaled some $44.1 billion – the single largest contributor to Canadian trade balance.

Canada is the world leader in sustainable forestry management practices. Only 120 million ha (28% of Canadian forests) are currently managed for timber production while an estimated 32 million ha are protected from harvesting by the current legislation.

USA

- *Cherry:* has a hardwood prized for its high quality in grain, width, colour, and rich warm glow. The first trees were carried to the lands surrounding Rome (Latium) from Armenia. In the United States, most cherry trees are grown in Washington, Pennsylvania, West Virginia, California and Oregon. When cherry tree flower, they make several among the most appreciated landscapes in Japan.
- *Cedar:* this genus are coniferas of the pinaceae family, originating from high mountain areas from Carpathians, Lebanon, Turkey to Himalaya. Their scented wood make them suitable for chests and closet lining. Cedar oil and wood is known to be a natural repellent to moths. Actually are planted in western and southern USA, mostly for ornamental purposes, but also for the production of pencils (specially incense-cedar).
- Douglas-fir: is a native tree of United State's west coast, with records in fast grow and the reaching of high statures in brief time. It has the ability to grow in mountains till the height of 1,800 meters. Their wood is used for construction, for homebuilt aircraft, for paper pulp, and also as firewood.
- Walnut: It is a prized furniture and carving hardwood because of its colour, hardness, grain and durability. Walnut wood has been the timber of choice for gun makers for centuries, including the Lee Enfield rifle. It remains one the most popular choices for rifle and shotgun stocks.

Caribbean and Central America

- Mahogany: has a straight grain, usually free of voids and pockets. The most prized species come from Cuba and Honduras. It has a reddish-brown color, which darkens over time, and displays a beautiful reddish sheen when polished. It has excellent workability, is available in big boards, and is very durable. Mahogany is used in the making of many musical instruments, as · drums, acoustic and electric guitars' back and side, and luxury headphones.

Europe

Italy

The species that are ideal for the many uses in this type of economy are those employed by arboriculture, that are very well known for their features and the need for certain types of ground and climates.

- *Fraxinus:* being a lightweight wood is easy to transport, as firewood burns easily, grows in damp environments like those present in river flooding areas, stands pollution of water and air.
- *Larix:* in Italy it grows at high altitudes around mountain tops, it's timber stand sudden climatic change, from icy winds to high temperatures in sunny afternoon summers, it's excellent to be used for the building of exposed structures as bridges, roofs, etc.
- *Stone pine:* "Mediterranean pine" could be the noble emblem of many coastal areas in Italy, originally giant forests of pines extended from the mouth of the Tiber river until Liguria and Provence in France, over soils with high salinity, not very apt for agriculture. It's trees produce a vast amount of dry branches that can be burnt, cones (used for Christmas decoration) and needle-like foliage that can be burnt, or used as mulch. Oils and resins can be used in scents and ointments. The pinoli are useful elements in Italian cooking (along with basil are tritured to make pesto sauce). Currently, "progress" has brought to a severe

reduction of this magnificent tree extensions, and in many places cheap beach buildings, car-parking and semi-abandoned areas have taken their place.

- *Poplar:* in Italy is the most important species for tree plantations, is used for several purposes as plywood manufacture, packing boxes, paper, matches, etc. It needs good quality grounds with good drainage, but can be used to protect the cultivations if disposed in windbreak lines. More than 70% of Italian poplar cultivations are located in the pianura Padana. Constantly the extension of the cultivation is being reduced, from 650 km^2 in the 80's to current 350 km^2. The yield of poplars is about 1,500 t/km^2 of wood every year. The production from poplars is around 45-50% of the total italian wood production.

  In the history of art poplar was the wood of choice for painting surfaces as panels, as in Renaissance (The Mona Lisa by Leonardo da Vinci). Because of this reason, many of the products with the highest added value, extremely expensive, are made with wood from the humble but durable poplar.

- Because of the presence of tannic acid, poplar cortex was often used in Europe for the tanning of leather.

Portugal

- *Oak for cork:* are trees with a slow growth, but long life, are cultivated in warm hill areas (min. temp. > -5°Celsius) in all the west area of Mediterranean shores. Popular for bulletin boards. Even if the production as stoppers for wine bottles is diminishing in favor of nylon stoppers, in the sake of energy saving granules of cork can be mixed into concrete. This composites have low thermal conductivity, low density and good energy absorption (earthquake resistant). Some of the property ranges of the composites are density (400–1500 kg/m^3), compressive strength (1–26 MPa) and flexural strength (0.5–4.0 MPa). Because of this cork can be used as thermal isolation in buildings (as well in it's natural form and as a mixture), useful also as sound insulation. In the shoe industry cork is used as soles and insoles. In the world there are 20,000 km^2 of cork oak plantations, and every year are extracted around 300,000 tons of cork, 50% in Portugal, 15,000 in Italy (12,000 in the island of Sardinia). The advantage of this natural industry is that the extraction of cork from layers outer to the cortex does not kills the tree.

- *Birch:* is a genus with many species of trees from Scandinavia and Russia, excellent for acid grounds. They act as pioneer species in the frozen border between taiga and tundra, are very resistant to periods of drought and icy conditions. The species Betula nana has been identified as the ideal tree for the acid grounds of the sides of sloped mountains, also in southern Europe, with soils poor in nutrients, where these trees can be used to restraint landslides. From birch tree can be extracted Xylitol, a natural sweetener.

USES OF WOOD

Combustion

Mean energy density of Wood, was calculated at around 6–17 Megajoule/Kilogram.

Charcoal

Direct Burning

The most intuitive use for wood, is that for burning in traditional fireplaces, even if combustion of wood is linked to the production of micro-environmental pollutants, as carbon dioxide (CO_2), and carbon monoxide (CO), an invisible gas able to provoke irreversible saturation of blood's hemoglobine, as well as nanoparticles.

In Italy poplar has been proposed as a tree cultivation to be transformed in biofuels, interesting because of the excellent ratio between the low energy needed to cultivate, cut and transport these trees, and the high amount of energy that can be extracted from it's wood, because poplar's capture of atmospheric carbon dioxide and their fast growing. As an example, *Populus euroamericana* clone "I-214", grows so fast that is able to reach 14 inches (35 cm) in diameter and heights of 100 feet (30 m) in ten years.

Wood Gasogen

Wood gas generator (gasogen): is a bulky and heavy device (but technically simple) that transforms burning wood in a mix of molecular hydrogen (H_2), carbon monoxide (CO), carbon dioxide (CO_2), molecular nitrogen (N_2) and water vapor (H_2O). This gas mixture, known as "poor gas" or "syngas" is obtained after the combustion of dry wood in a reductive environment (low in oxygen) with a limited amount of atmospheric air, at temperatures of 900° Celsius, through an internal combustion engine.

In the time between World War I and World War II included, because of the lack of oil, in many countries, like Italy, France, Great Britain and Sweden, several gasoline-powered cars were modified, with the addition of a wood gas generator (a "*gasogen*"), a device powered by wood, coal, or burnable waste, able to produce (and purify) gas that immediately, in the same vehicle, could power a slightly modified ICE engine of a standard car (low-compression engine). Carburetor had to be changed with an air-gas mixer). There were several setbacks, as the great reduction of maximum speed and the need to drive using low gears and wisely dosing the amount of air. In modern cars, modified with a wood gas generator, gas emissions (CO, CO_2 and NOx) are lower to those of the same vehicle running with gasoline (keeping the same catalytic converter).

Methanol

Methanol, also known as *formic alcohol* (H_3C-OH), is the simplest alcohol (an hydroxyl radical bonded to a molecule of methane), which behaves as a liquid at 25° C, is very toxic (lethal) and corrosive, and in organic chemistry basic books is often called "the spirit of wood", since it can be obtained from wood fermentation. Rarely, when unwise wine-makers mix small chunks of wood and leaves with grapes, methanol can be found as a pollutant of the blend of water, ethanol and other substances derived from grape's fermentation.

Best way to obtain methanol from wood is through syngas (CO, CO_2, H_2) produced by the anhydrous pyrolysis of wood, a method discovered by ancient egyptians.

Methanol can be used as an oxygen-rich additive for gasoline, but ussually it is much cheaper to produce it from methane or from syngas, and it is the most important base material for industrial chemistry, where it is often used to make more complex molecules, through reactions of halogenation and later by chemical addition reaction.

Gas Turbine

Construction

Wood is relatively light in weight, because it's specific weight is less than 500 kg/m^3, this is an advantage, when compared against 2,000-2,500 kg/m^3 for armed concrete or 7,800 kg/m^3 for steel.

Is strong, becausee the efficiency of wood for structural purposes has qualities that are similar to steel.

Briges, Levees, Microhydro, Piers

Wood is used to build bridges (as the Magere bridge in Amsterdam), as well as water and air mills, and microhydro generators for electricity.

Housing

Plywood

Plywood is a type of engineered board made from thin sheets of wood , called plies or wood veneers. The layers are glued together, each with its grain at right angles to adjacent layers for greater strength. There are usually an odd number of plies, as the symmetry makes the board less prone to warping and the grain on the outside surfaces runs in the same direction. plies are bonded under heat and pressure with strong adhesives, usually phenol formaldehyde resin,[making plywood a type of composite material. Plywood is sometimes called the original en.

The adhesives used in plywood has become a point of concern, dueto the off gassing of the formaldehyde. Both urea formaldehyde and phenol formaldehyde are carcinogenic, so their use undesirable. Many manufacturers are turning to "Greener Products" as government regulations become stronger against the use of these adhesives.

A common reason for using plywood instead of plain wood is its resisance to cracking, shrinkage, twisting/warping, and its general high egree of strength. It has replaced many dimensional lumbers on construction applications for these reasons.

Types of Plywood

A vast number of varieties of plywood exist for different applications. Softwood plywood is usually made either of Douglas fir or spruce, pine, and fir, and is typically used for construction and industrial purposes. Decorative plywood is usually faced with hardwood, including red oak, birch, maple, lauan (Philippine mahogany) and a large number of other hardwoods.

Plywood for indoor use generally uses the less expensive urea-fomaldehyde glue which has limited water resistance, while outdoorand marine grade plywood are designed to withstand rot, and use a water resistant phenol-formaldehyde glue to prevent delamination and to retain strength in high humidity.

The most common varieties of softwood plywood come in three, five or seven plies with a metric dimension of 1.2 m × 2.4 m or the slightly larger imperial dimension of 4 feet × 8 feet. Plies vary in thickness from 1/10" through 1/6" depending on the panel thickness. Roofing can use the thinner 5/8-inch plywood. Subfloors are at least 3/4-inch depending on the distance between floor joists. Plywood for flooring applications is often tongue and grooved. The mating edge will have a "groove" notched into it to fit with the adjacent "tongue" that protrudes from the next board. This keeps the boards from slipping past each other providing a solid feeling floor when the joints do not lie over joists. Tongue and groove flooring plywood is typically 1" in thickness.

High-strength plywood, known as aircraft plywood, is made from mahogany and/or birch, and uses adhesives with increased resistance to heat and humidity. It was used for several

World War II fighter aircraft, including the British-built Mosquito bomber which was nicknamed the wooden wonder.

Certain plywoods do not have alternating plies. These are designed for a specific purpose. One such plywood is known as "Bendy Board". This is very flexible and is designed for making curved parts.

Other types of plywoods are fire retardant, moisture resistant, marine grade, sign grade, pressure treated, and of course the hardwood and softwood plywoods. Each of these products are designed to fill a need in industry.

In addition to the glues being brought to the forefront, the wood resources themselves are becoming the focus of manufacturers, due in part to energy conservation, as well as concern for our natural resources. There are several certifications available to manufacturers who participate in these programmes. FSC certified, Leeds Certified, FSI certified, and Greenguard certified. Many of these programmes offer tax benefits to both the manufacturer, as well as the end user.

Plywood Production

Plywood production requires a good log, called a peeler, which is generally straighter and larger in diameter than one required for processing into dimensioned lumber by a sawmill. The log is peeled into sheets of veneer which are then cut to the desired dimensions, dried, patched, glued together and then baked in a press at 140 °C (280 °F) and 19 MPa (2800 psi) to form the plywood panel. The panel can then be patched, resized, sanded or otherwise refinished, depending on the market for which it is intended.

Plywood has been made for thousands of years; the earliest known occurrence of plywood was in Ancient Egypt around 3500 BCE when wooden articles were made from sawn veneers glued together crosswise. This was originally done due to a shortage of fine wood. Thin sheets of high quality wood were glued over a substrate of lower quality wood for cosmetic effect, with incidental structural benefits. This manner of inventing plywood has occurred repeatedly throughout history. Most high quality

English furniture makers working in the eighteenth and nineteenth centuries (and since) have used veneering as a technique. In addition to making the most out of the highest quality materials available, it reduces prices and improves stability of construction. The irregularities of grain which confer decorative interest often result in uncontrollable warping and cracking if any attempt is made to use the wood in thicknesses much greater than those characterizing cabinet-making veneers (typically 1-2mm).

Modern plywood, in which the veneer is cut on a rotary lathe from softwood logs, is of relatively recent origin, invented by Immanuel Nobel. The first such lathes were set up in the United States in the mid 19th century. Plywood has been one of the most ubiquitous building products for decades.

One of the earliest applications of mass-produced modern plywood manufacturing in the United States was recorded in Portland, Oregon by the Portland Manufacturing Company. The owner, helped develop a bonding technology, which greatly shortened the drying and manufacturing process. His early engineering contribution played an important role in making plywood one of the most abundant and affordable building products ever produced.

In India, waterproof plywood is also known as "kitply". Though Kitply is a brand, it has become a genericized trademark, since the company that makes it pioneered the use of waterproof plywood in India.

The landscape historian John Stilgoe has theorized that the 4' x 8' dimensions of a standard sheet are due to the space required for moving a mule into a barn .

Plywood Advantages

1. *High uniform strength:* Wood is 45 times stronger along the grain than across the grain. Crossing the adjacent sheets tends to equalise the strength in all directions.

2. *Freedom from shrinking, swelling and warping:* Solid wood exhibits considerable movement across the grain but generally negligible shrinkage or swelling in a longitudinal

plane. The balanced construction of a plywood panel with the grain direction of adjacent veneers at right angles tends to equalise stress, thus reducing shrinkage, swelling and warping.

3. *Non-splitting qualities:* Solid wood splits fairly readily along the grain. Plywood by virtue of the crossed laminations can be nailed or screwed near the edges without damage from splitting.

4. *Availability of relatively large sizes:* Sawn timber can be obtained in fairly long lengths but only in relatively narrow widths. Plywood can be sold in sizes up to 6 ft * 25 ft and by the scarf jointing of small sheets up to 6 ft *40 ft, however 8 ft*4 ft is the most common size.

5. *Economical and effective utilisation of figured wood:* Twenty sheets of veneer can be sliced from 1 inch of solid wood. When glued to a core of cheaper material a high grade panel is produced. This procedure thus affects distinct economies in the use of figured or the more valuable woods. In addition to facilitating the utilisation of attractive but fragile face veneers to give results which cannot be duplicated in solid construction. More effective utilisation is obtained by the matching of veneer in such a manner that the decorative effect due to the natural figure in the wood is enhanced by the regularity or symmetry of the design.

6. *Ease of fabrication of curved surfaces:* The trend of modern architectural design is to feature curved surfaces. The desired shapes can be readily fabricated in plywood construction, utilising male and female forms, or a single forming a vacuum press or autoclave.

7. *Reduction of waste:* One of the important aspects in the manufacture of plywood is that it results in the conservation of timber by the elimination of the waste which occurs in sawing e.g. sawdust. Waste is confined to the small core which remains after peeling, from the veneer which is lost in rounding up the log, and the elimination of such defects as knots and splits.

8. Dense woods can be sliced and bonded into plywood panels for use in furniture construction whereas furniture fabricated from solid timber would be far too heavy.

US Plywood Grades

Plywood grades are determined by a veneer quality on the face and back of each panel. The first letter designates quality of face veneer (best side), while the second letter denotes the surface quality of the back of the panel. The letter "X" indicates the panel was manufactured with scrap wood as the center plies, not "exterior" as is commonly thought. The A-D rating is only good for construction (softwood) plywood, not for hardwood plywoods such as oak or maple.

"A": Highest grade quality available. Can be defect free or contain small knots, providing they are replaced with wooden plugs (the fillers having a "boat" or an "American football" shape) or repaired with synthetic patch. This grade may contain occasional surface splits that are repaired with synthetic filler. The surface is always sanded and provides for smooth paintable face quality.

"B": Second highest quality veneer grade. Normally a by-product of downgraded "A" quality veneer. Solid surface, but may contain small diameter knots and narrow surface splits. Normally repaired with wooden plugs or synthetic filler. The surface is normally sanded smooth.

"C": Considered to be a lower end face quality, but a reasonable choice for general construction purposes. May contain tight knots up to 1½ inches diameter, some open knot holes, some face splits, and discoloration. Some manufactures may repair the defects with synthetic filler. Panels are typically not sanded.

"D": Considered to be the lowest quality veneer and often used for the back surface for construction grade panels. Allows for several knots, large and small, as well as open knots up to 2½ inches diameter. Open knots, splits, and discoloration are acceptable. "D" grade veneers are neither repaired nor sanded. This grade is not recommended for permanent exposure to weather elements.

Plywood is used in many applications that need high-quality, high-strength sheet material. Quality in this context means resistance to cracking, breaking, shrinkage, twisting and warping. Plywood is also used as an engineering material for stressed-skin applications. It has been used for marine and aviation applications since WWII. Most notable is the British De Havilland Mosquito bomber, which was primarily made out of wood. Plywood is currently successfully used in stressed-skin applications. . The American designers Charles and Ray Eames and Phil Bolger are famous for their plywood-based furniture.

WOOD PRESERVATION

All measures that are taken to ensure a long life of wood fall under the definition wood preservation (timber treatment). Apart from structural wood preservation measures, there are a number of different (chemical) preservatives and processes (also known as timber treatment or lumber treatment) that can extend the life of wood, timber, wood structures or engineered wood. These generally increase the durability and resistance from being destroyed by insects or fungus.

A modern wharf piling bored by bivalves known as "shipworms".

As proposed by Richardson, treatment of wood has been practised for almost as long as the use of wood itself. Some accounts reach back to the beginning of recorded history. For example the Bible in Genesis, 6:13-14 "And God said unto Noah . . . make thee an ark of gopher wood; rooms shalt thou make in the ark, and shalt pitch it within and without with pitch." There are also records of wood preservation reaching back to ancient Greece during Alexander the Great's rule, where bridge wood was soaked in olive oil. The Romans also protected their wood by brushing their ship hulls with tar. During the Industrial Revolution wood preservation became a corner stone of the wood processing industry. Inventors and scientists such as Bethell, Boucherie, Burnett and Kyan made historic developments in wood preservation, with the preservative solutions and processes.

Old timber industrially treated with approved preservative products should pose no greater threat to the public than untreated timber. Industrial wood preservation chemicals are generally not available directly to the public and may require special approval to import or purchase depending on the product and the jurisdiction where being used. In most countries, industrial wood preservation operations are notifiable industrial activities that require licensing from relevant regulatory authorities such as EPA or equivalent. Reporting and licensing conditions vary widely depending on the particular chemicals used and the country of use.

Unfortunately previous poor practices in industry have left legacies of contaminated ground and water around wood treatment operation sites in a number of cases. However under currently approved industry practices and regulatory controls such as implemented in Europe, North America, Australia, New Zealand, Japan and elsewhere, environmental impact of these operations should be minimal.

Wood treated with modern preservatives is generally safe to handle given appropriate handling precautions and personal protection measures. However, treated wood may present certain hazards in some circumstances such as during combustion or where wood dust or other fine residues are generated or where treated wood comes into direct contact with food and agriculture.

Material safety data sheets and safe handling guidelines are required by law to be provided by suppliers of wood preservative chemicals and treated wood products. This information should be obtained and reviewed before handling and using wood preservative chemicals and treated wood products.

Chemical Preservatives

Timber or lumber that is treated with a preservative generally have it applied through vacuum and/or pressure treatment. The preservatives used to pressure-treat timber are classified as pesticides. Treating timber provides long-term resistance to organisms that cause deterioration. If it is applied correctly, it extends the productive life of timber by five to ten times. If left untreated, wood that is exposed to moisture or soil for sustained periods of time will become weakened by various types of fungi, bacteria or insects.

Chemical preservatives can be classified into three broad categories: Water-borne salts, Oil-borne preservatives, and Light Organic Solvent Preservatives (LOSPs). These are discussed in more detail below.

Water-borne Preservatives

Water is the most common solvent carrier in preservative formulations due to its availability and low cost. Water-bourne systems do however have the drawback that they swell timber, leading to increased twisting, splitting and checking than alternatives.

Chromated Copper Arsenate (CCA)

An extremely common preservative originally developed in the 1930s at the Forest Research Institute in Dehra Dun, India, by Dr Sonti Kamesam. Dr Kamesam sold the patent rights for what he originally called ASCU salts to the Bell Telephone Company of the USA. The acronym "CCA" is believed to have come into popular use for this product in the 1950s. In CCA treatment, copper is the primary fungicide, arsenic is a secondary fungicide and an insecticide, and chromium is a fixative which also provides ultraviolet (UV) light resistance. Recognized for the greenish tint it imparts to timber, CCA is a preservative that was extremely common for many decades; however, it contained arsenic.

Pressure treatment with an aqueous solution of CCA salts is often known in the UK as Tanalisation. The chemicals are applied using a vacuum and pressure cycle, and the treated wood is then stacked to dry. During the process, the mixture of salts reacts to form insoluble compounds, helping with leaching problems. If the process is carried out correctly, very little preservative is left on the surface of the wood, and the safety hazard from surface toxins is minimised. Occasionally, a white powdery deposit may be seen on the surface; this is either hydrated-sodium sulphate, a harmless by-product of the CCA salts, or some resin that has exuded from the wood during treatment. Both these deposits are easily removed by scrubbing or brushing, and such treatment will also reduce the minimal amounts of arsenic, which may be present on the surface of the wood.

In the last decade concerns were raised that the chemicals may leach from the wood into surrounding soil, resulting in concentrations higher than naturally occurring background levels. A study cited in *Forest Products Journal* found 12–13% of the chromated copper arsenate leached from treated wood buried in compost during a 12-month period. Once these chemicals have leached from the wood, they are likely to bind to soil particles, especially in soils with clay or soils that are more alkaline than neutral. In the United States the powerful US Consumer Product Safety Commission issued a report in 2002 stating that exposure to arsenic from direct human contact with CCA treated wood may be higher than was previously thought. On 1 January 2004 the Environmental Protection Agency (EPA) in a voluntary agreement with industry began restricting the use of CCA in treated timber in residential and commercial construction, with the exception of shakes and shingles, permanent wood foundations, and certain commercial applications. This was in an effort to reduce the use of arsenic and improve environmental safety, although the EPA were careful to point out that they had not concluded that CCA treated wood structures in service posed an unacceptable risk to the community. The EPA did not call for the removal or dismantling of existing CCA treated wood structures.

In Australia, the Australian Pesticides and Veterinary Medicines Authority (APVMA restricted the use of CCA preservative for treatment of timber used in certain applications from March 2006. CCA may no longer be used to treat wood used in 'intimate human contact' applications such as children's play equipment, furniture, residential decking and handrailing. Use for low contact residential, commercial and industrial applications remains unrestricted, as does its use in all other situations. The APVMA decision to restrict the use of CCA in Australia was a precautionary measure, even though the report found no evidence that demonstrated CCA treated timber posed unreasonable risks to humans in normal use. Similarly to the US EPA, the APVMA did not recommend dismantling or removal of existing CCA treated wood structures.

In Europe, Directive 2003/2/EC restricts the marketing and use of arsenic, including CCA wood treatment. CCA treated wood is not permitted to be used in residential or domestic constructions. It is permitted for use in various industrial and public works, such as bridges, highway safety fencing, electric power transmission and telecommunications poles.

Alkaline Copper Quaternary

Alkaline copper quaternary (ACQ) is a preservative made up of copper, a fungicide, and a quaternary ammonium compound (quat), an insecticide which also augments the fungicidal treatment is a wood preservative that has come into wide use in the USA, Europe, Japan and Australia following restrictions on CCA. Its use is governed by national and international standards, which determine the volume of preservative uptake required for a specific timber end use.

Since it contains high levels of copper, ACQ-treated timber is five times more corrosive to common steel, according to American Wood Preservers Association (AWPA) test results. It is necessary to use double-galvanized or stainless steel fasteners in ACQ timber. Use of fasteners meeting or exceeding requirements for ASTM A 153 Class D meet the added requirements for fastener durability. The U.S. began mandating the use of non-arsenic containing wood preservatives for virtually all residential use timber in 2004.

Modern versions have been developed which offer improved performance to those mentioned above. It should be noted that the American Wood Protection Association (AWPA) standards for ACQ require a retention of 0.25 pounds per cubic ft (PCF) for above ground use and .40 pcf for ground contact. Check the label and beware that some dealers are offering ACQ products with sub-standard retentions, these sub-standard retentions should not be used in applications where AWPA standard products are specified and consumers should consider the risks of using sub-standard retentions in long-term mission critical applications.

Chemical Specialties, Inc (CSI, now Viance) received US EPA's Presidential Green Chemistry Challenge Award in 2002 for commercial introduction of ACQ. Its widespread use has eliminated major quantities of arsenic and chromium previously contained in CCA.

Copper Azole

Copper azole preservative (denoted as CA-B under American Wood Protection Association (AWPA) standards) is the other major copper based wood preservative that has come into wide use in the USA, Europe, Japan and Australia following restrictions on CCA. Its use is governed by national and international standards, which determine the volume of preservative uptake required for a specific timber end use.

Copper Azole is similar to ACQ with the difference being that the dissolved copper preservative is augmented by an Azole co-biocide instead of the quat biocide used in ACQ. The Azole co-biocide yields a Copper Azole product that is effective at much lower retentions than required for equivalent ACQ performance.

It is marketed exclusively under the "Wolmanized" brand in the US, and the "Tanalith" brand across Europe and other international markets. Many companies treating with ACQ treatments attempt to piggyback the success of this brand by describing ACQ treated timber as "Tanalised", which is a registered trade mark infringement.

The AWPA standard retention for CA-B is .10 pounds per cubic ft (pcf) for above ground applications and .21 pcf for ground contact applications. Recently a new version of copper azole, denoted as CA-C, has been introduced under the Wolmanized brand. CA-C has been submitted to the AWPA for evaluation and acceptance as a new AWPA standard with retentions of .06 pounds per cubic ft (pcf) for above ground applications and .15 pcf for ground contact applications. AWPA acceptance is expected in due course.

The copper azole preservative incorporates organic triazoles such as tebuconazole or propiconazole as the co-biocide, which are also used to protect food crops. The general appearance of wood treated with copper azole preservative is similar to CCA with a green colouration.

Other Copper Compounds

These include copper HDO (CuHDO), copper chromate, copper citrate, acid copper chromate and ammoniacal copper zinc arsenate (ACZA). The CuHDO treatment is an alternative to CCA, ACQ and CA used in Europe and in approval stages for United States and Canada. AZCA is generally used for marine applications.

Micronized Copper Technology

sems, MCQ marketed as MicroPro, is the only preservative technology to achieve Environmentally Preferable Product Certification. This "EPP" Certification was issued by Scientific Certifications Systems (SCS) in December 2007 and is based on a comparative Life Cycle Impact Assessment with an industry standard. However, as of February 2008 no report has been made public documenting the methods, assumptions and inputs used in the analysis.

Borate Preservatives

Boric acid, oxides and salts (borates) are effective wood preservatives ground contact. Recent interest in low toxicity timber for residential use, along with new regulations restricting some wood preservation agents, has resulted in a resurgence of the use of borate treated wood for floor beams and internal structural members.

Sodium Silicate-based Preservatives

Sodium silicate is produced by fusing sodium with sand or heating bot ood by moisture, forming a flake-like layer on top of the wood. One company, Timber Treatment Technology, LLC, has found that infusing timber with a chemical solution containing sodium silicate with a specified energy level applied yields wood that not only does not provide flake or layering on the wood, nor does it wash out as others have done in the past; and it provides processed timber that received a class A fire classification. Their processed wood also paints and stains as new wood does. TTT, LLC, sells these products under the name TimberSIL. Other uses include fixing pigments in paintings and cloth printing, and for preserving eggs.

Potassium Silicate-based Preservatives

There are a number of European "natural" paint fabricants that have developed potassium silicate (potassium waterglass) based preservatives. They are frequently include boron compounds, cellulose, lignin and other plant extracts. They are a surface application with a minimal impregnation for internal use.

Bifenthrin Spray Preservatives

In Australia, a water-based bifenthrin preservative has been developed to improve the insect resistance of timber. As this preservative is applied by spray, it only penetrates the outer 2mm of the timber cross-section. Concerns have been raised as to whether this thin-envelope system will provide protection against insects in the longer term, particularly when exposed to sunlight for extended periods.

Fire Retardant Treated

This treated wood contains a fire retardant chemical that remains stable in high temperature environments and does not increase the corrosivity of metal hardware in contact with the wood. Also use baden

Oil-borne Preservatives

These include pentachlorophenol and creosote. They are toxic, have an unpleasant odour and are generally not used in consumer products.

Coal-tar Creosote

Creosote is a tar-based preservative that has been commonly used for telephone poles and railroad ties. Creosote is one of the oldest wood preservatives, and was originally derived from a wood distillate. These days virtually all creosote is manufactured from the distillation of coal tar. It often collects inside chimneys and may cause a fire hazard. Creosote is regulated as a pesticide and is not usually sold to the general public. It is still used for railway sleepers and utility poles.

Linseed Oil

In recent years in Australia and New Zealand, Linseed has been incorporated in preservative formulations as a solvent and water repellent to 'envelope treat' timber. This involves just treating the outer 5mm of the cross-section of a timber member with preservative eg Permethrin 25:75, leaving the core-untreated. While not as effective as CCA or LOSP methods, envelope treatments are significantly cheaper as they use far less preservative. Major preservative manufacturers add a blue dye to envelope treatments. There is an on-going promotional campaign in Australia for this type of treatment. Linseed oil is used to preserve Wood fences, log cabins, and wood furniture. (Such woods as Willow, Pine, oak and exc.) The function of linseed oil as a preservative is believed to be related to its action as a water repellent and drying agent rather than a direct biocidal activity. A number of European companies have developed natural-oil-only-based treatments; no synthetic preservative such as permethrin is added. Menz Holz OHT use autoclave impregnation with linseed, sunflower and rapeseed oil for 6 to 8 hours.

Other Emulsions

Light Organic Solvent Preservatives (LOSP)

This class of timber treatments use white spirit as the solvent carrier to deliver preservative compounds into timber. Synthetic pyrethroids are used as an insecticide, such as permethrin, bifenthrin or deltamethrin. In Australia and New Zealand, the most common formulations use Permethrin as an insecticide, and Propaconazole & Tebuconazole as fungicides. While still using a chemical preservative, this formulation contains no heavy-metal compounds.

With the introduction of strict volatile organic compound (VOC) laws in the European Union, LOSPs have disadvantages due to the high cost and long process times associated with vapour-recovery systems. LOSPs have been emulsified into water-based solvents. While this does significantly reduce VOC emissions, the timber swells during treatment, removing many of the advantages of LOSP formulations.

New Technologies

Wood Acetylation

Chemical modification of wood at the molecular level has been used to improve its performance properties. Many chemical reaction systems for the modification of wood, especially those using various types of anhydrides, have been published; however, the reaction of wood with acetic anhydride has been the most studied.

The physical properties of any material are determined by its chemical structure. Wood contains an abundance of chemical groups called "free hydroxyls". Free hydroxyl groups readily absorb and release water according to changes in the climatic conditions to which they are exposed. This is the main reason why wood's dimensional stability is impacted by swelling and shrinking. It is also believed that the digestion of wood by enzymes initiates at the free hydroxyl sites - which is one of the principal reasons why, wood is prone to decay.

Acetylation effectively changes the free hydroxyls within wood into acetyl groups. This is done by reacting the wood with acetic anhydride, which comes from acetic acid (known as vinegar when in its dilute form). When free hydroxyl groups are transformed to acetyl groups, the ability of the wood to absorb water is greatly reduced, rendering the wood more dimensionally stable and, because it is no longer digestible, extremely durable. In general, softwoods naturally have an acetyl content between 0.5 to 1.5% and more durable hardwoods between 2 to 4.5%. Acetylation takes wood well beyond these levels with corresponding benefits. These include an extended coatings life due to acetylated wood acting as a more stable substrate for paints and translucent coatings. Acetylated wood is non-toxic and does not have the environmental issues associated with traditional preservation techniques.

The acetylation of wood was first done in Germany in 1928 by Fuchs. In 1946, Tarkow, Stamm and Erickson first described the use of wood acetylation to stabilize wood from swelling in water. Since the 1940's, many laboratories around the world have looked at acetylation of many different types of woods and agricultural resources.

In spite of the vast amount of research on chemical modification of wood, and, more specifically, on the acetylation of wood, commercialization did not come easily. The first patent on the acetylation of wood was filed by Suida in Austria in 1930. Later, in 1947, Stamm and Tarkow filed a patent on the acetylation of wood and boards using pyridine as a catalyst. In 1961, the Koppers Company published a technical bulletin on the acetylation of wood using no catalysis but with an organic cosolvent In 1977, in Russia, Otlesnov and Nikitina came close to commercialization but the process was discontinued presumably because cost-effectiveness could not be achieved. In 2007 a London-based company, with production facilities in The Netherlands, achieved cost-effective commercialization and began large-scale production of acetylated wood.

Natural Preservatives

Naturally Rot-resistant Woods

This includes Western Redcedar, Huon Pine, Merbau, Ironbark, many cypresses and Coast Redwood. These species are resistant to decay in their natural state, due to high levels of organic chemicals called "extractives", mainly polyphenols. Extractives are chemicals that are deposited in the heartwood of certain tree species as they convert sapwood to heartwood. However, many of these species tend to be prohibitively expensive for general construction applications.

Huon pine was used for ship hulls in the 19th century, but overharvesting and huon pine's extremely slow growth rate makes this now a specialty timber. Merbau is still a popular decking timber and has a long life in above ground applications, but it is considered unsustainably logged (see Illegal logging) and is too hard and brittle for general use. Huon pine is so rot resistant that fallen trees from many years ago are still commercially valuable. Ironbark is a good choice where available. It is harvested from both old-growth and plantation in Australia and is highly resistant to rot and termites. It is most commonly used for fence posts and house stumps.

Eastern red cedar and black locust have long been used for rot-resistant fence posts and rails in eastern United States, with the black locust also planted in modern times in Europe. Redwood is commonly used for similar applications in the western United States. It should be noted that the natural durability or rot and insect resistance of wood species is always based on the heartwood (or truewood). The sapwood of all timber species should be considered to be non-durable without preservative treatment.

Tung Oil

Tung oil has been known about for hundreds of years in China, where it was used as a preservative for wood ships. The oil penetrates the wood, then hardens to form an impermeable hydrophobic layer up to 5 mm into the wood. As a preservative it is effective for exterior work above and below ground, but the thin layer makes it less useful in practice. It is not available as a pressure treatment. Some manufacturers recommend tung oil as a stabiliser for CCA.

Heat Treatments

There is ongoing research as to whether heat treatments can be used to make timber more durable. By heating timber to a certain temperature, it may be possible to make the wood-fibre less appetising to insects. Although unlikely to be as effective as chemical preservatives, anecdotal evidence suggests some consumers would prefer chemical-free timber preservation methods.

Heat treatment can also improve the properties of the wood with respect to water: lower equilibrium moisture, less moisture deformation, and weather resistance. It is weather-resistant enough to be used, unprotected, in facades or in kitchen tables, where wetting is expected.

There are three similar European heat treatments Retiwood developed in France, Thermowood developed in Finland by VTT and Platowood developed in The Netherlands. All process's use autoclave pressure + heat, and nitrogen or water vapour to control drying in a staged treatment process ranging from 24 to 48 hours at temperatures of 180 à 230°C depending on timber species. All increase the durability, dimensional stability and hardness by at least one class. The timber is darkened in colour and there is a reduction in the mechanical properties of the timber ; modulus of elasticity increased 0 to 10%, modulus of rupture diminished by 5 to 20% e.g. timber requires drilling for nailing otherwise it may split. Not all process's are equal in their reduction of mechanical properties. Timber used for cladding, flooring, furniture and windows are treated with this process.

Application Processes

Probably the first attempts made to protect wood from decay and insect attack consisted of brushing or rubbing preservatives onto the surfaces of the treated wood. Through trial and error the most effective preservatives and application processes where slowly determined. In the Industrial Revolution, demands for such things as telegraph poles and railroad ties helped to fuel an explosion of new techniques that emerged in the early 19th century. The sharpest rise in inventions took place between 1830 and 1840, when Bethell, Boucherie, Burnett and Kyan were making wood-preserving history. Since then, numerous processes have been introduced or existing processes improved. The goal of modern day wood preservation is to ensure a deep, uniform penetration with reasonable cost, without endangering the environment. The most widespread application processes today are those using artificial pressure through which many woods are being effectively treated, but several species (such as Spruce, Douglas Fir, Larch, Hemlock and Fir) are very resistant to impregnation. With the use of incising, the treatment of these woods has been somewhat successful but with a higher cost and not always satisfactory results. One can divide the wood-preserving methods roughly into either non-pressure processes or pressure processes.

Non-pressure Processes

There are numerous non-pressure processes of treating wood which vary primarily in their procedure. The most common of these treatments involve the application of the preservative by means of brushing or spraying, dipping, soaking, steeping or by means of hot and cold bath. There is also a variety of additional methods involving charring, applying preservatives in bored holes, diffusion processes and sap displacement.

Brush and Spray Treatments

Brushing preservatives is a long-practiced method and often used in today's carpentry workshops. Through technology developments it is also possible to spray preservative over the surface of the timber. Some of the liquid is drawn into the wood as the result of capillary action, but this penetration is insignificant and not suitable for long-term weathering. By using the spray method, coal-tar creosote, oil-borne solutions and water-borne salts (to some extent) can also be applied. A thorough brush or spray treatment with coal-tar creosote can add 1 to 3 years to the lifespan of poles or posts. Two or more coats provide better protection than one, but the successive coats should not be applied until the prior coat has dried or soaked into the wood. The wood should be seasoned before treatment.

Dipping

Dipping consists of simply immersing the wood in a bath of creosote or other preservative for a few seconds or minutes. Similar penetrations to that of brushing and spraying processes are achieved. It has the advantage of minimizing hand labor. It requires more equipment and larger quantities of preservative and is not adequate for treating small lots of timber. Usually the dipping process is useful in the treatment of window sashes and doors. Treatment with Copper salt preservatives is no longer allowed with this method.

Steeping

In this process the wood is submerged in a tank of water-preservative mix, and allowed to soak for a longer period of time (several days to weeks). This process was developed in the 19th century by John Kyan. The depth and retention achieved depends on factors such as species, wood moisture, preservative and soak duration. The majority of the absorption takes place during the first two or three days, but will continue at a slower pace for an indefinite period. As a result, the longer the wood can be left in the solution, the better treatment it will receive. When treating seasoned timber, both the water and the preservative salt soak into the wood, making it necessary to season the wood a second time. Posts and poles can be treated directly on endangered areas, but should be treated at least 30 cm (1 ft) above the future ground level.

The depth obtained during regular steeping periods varies from 5 mm to 10 mm (1/8 to 1/3 in.) up to 30 mm (1 in.) by sap pine. Due to the low absorption, solution strength should be somewhat stronger than that in pressure processes, around 5% for seasoned timber and 10% for green timber (because the concentration slowly decreases as the chemicals diffuse into the wood). The solution strength should be controlled continually and, if necessary, be corrected with the salt additive. After the timber is removed from the treatment tank, the chemical will continue to spread within the wood if it has sufficient moisture content. The wood should be weighed down and piled so that the solution can reach all surfaces. (Sawed materials stickers should be placed between every board layer.) This process finds minimal use despite its former popularity in continental Europe and Great Britain.

Kyanizing

Named after John Howard Kyan, who patented this process in England in 1832, Kyanizing consists of steeping wood in a 0.67% mercuric chloride preservative solution.

Hot and Cold Bath

Patented by C.A. Seeley, this process achieves treatment by immersing seasoned wood in successive baths of hot and cold preservatives. During the hot baths, the air expands in the timbers. When the timbers are changed to the cold bath (the preservative can also be changed) a partial vacuum is created within the lumen of the cells, causing the preservative to be drawn into the wood. Some penetration occurs during the hot baths, but most of it takes place during the cold baths. This cycle is repeated with a significant time reduction compared to other steeping processes. Each bath may last 4 to 8 hours or in some cases longer. The temperature of the preservative in the hot bath should be between 60 to 110 °C (140 to 225 °F) and 30 to 40 °C (85 to 105 °F) in the cold bath (depending on preservative and treespecies). The average penetration depths achieved with this process ranges from 30 mm to 50 mm (1 to 12/3 in.). Both preservative oils and water-soluble salts can be used with this treatment. Due to the longer treatment periods, this method finds little use in the commercial wood preservation industry today.

Pressure Processes

Pressure processes are the most permanent method around today in preserving timber life. Pressure processes are those in which the treatment is carried out in closed cylinders with applied pressure and/or vacuum. These processes have a number of advantages over the non-pressure methods. In most cases, a deeper and more uniform penetration and a higher absorption of preservative is achieved. Another advantage is that the treating conditions can be controlled so that retention and penetration can be varied. These pressure processes can be adapted to large-scale production. The high initial costs for equipment and the energy costs are the biggest disadvantages. These treatment methods are used to protect ties, poles and structural timbers and find use throughout the world today. The various pressure processes that are used today differ in details, but the general method is in all cases the same. The treatment is carried out in cylinders. The timbers are loaded onto special tram cars, so called "buggies," and into the cylinder. These cylinders are then set under pressure often with the addition of higher temperature. As final treatment, a vacuum is frequently used to extract excess preservatives. These cycles can be repeated to achieve better penetration.

LOSP treatments often use a vacuum impregnation process. This is possible because of the lower viscosity of the white-spirit carrier used.

Full-cell Process

In the full-cell process, the intent is to keep as much of the liquid absorbed into the wood during the pressure period as possible, thus leaving the maximum concentration of preservatives in the treated area. Usually, water solutions of preservative salts are employed with this process but it is also possible to impregnate wood with oil. The desired retention is achieved by changing the strength of the solution. William

Burnett patented this development in 1838 of Full-Cell Impregnation with water solutions. The patent covered the use of zinc chloride on water basis, also known as Burnettizing. Full-Cell Process with oils was patented in 1838 by John Bethell. His patent described the injection of tar and oils into wood by applying pressure in closed cylinders. This process is still used today with some improvements.

Fluctuation Pressure Process

Contrary to the "static" Full-Cell and Empty-Cell processes, the Fluctuation Process is a "dynamic" Process. By this process the pressure inside the impregnation cylinder changes between pressure and vacuum within a few seconds. There have been inconsistent claims that through this process it is possible to reverse the pit closure by Spruce. However the best results that have been achieved with this process by Spruce do not exceed a penetration deeper than 10 mm (1/3in.). Specialized equipment is necessary and therefore higher investment costs are incurred.

Boucherie Process

Developed by Dr. Boucherie of France in 1838, this approach consisted of attaching a bag or container of preservative solution to a standing or a freshly cut tree with bark, branches, and leaves still attached, thereby injecting the liquid into the sap stream. Through transpiration of moisture from the leaves the preservative is drawn upward through the sapwood of the tree trunk.

The modified Boucherie process consists of placing freshly cut, unpeeled timbers onto declining skids, with the stump slightly elevated, then fastening watertight covering caps or boring a number of holes into the ends, and inserting a solution of copper sulfate or other water- borne preservative into the caps or holes from an elevated container. Preservative oils tend to not penetrate satisfactorily by this method. The hydrostatic pressure of the liquid forces the preservative lengthwise into and through the sapwood, thus pushing the sap out of the other end of the timber. After a few days, the sapwood is completely impregnated; unfortunately little or no penetration takes place in the heartwood. Only green wood can be treated in this manner. This process has found considerable usage to impregnate poles and also larger trees in Europe and North America, and has experienced a revival of usage to impregnate bamboo in countries such as Costa Rica, Bangladesh, India and the state of Hawaii.

High Pressure Sap Displacement System

Developed in the Philippines, this method (abbreviated HPSD) consists of a cylinder pressure cap made from a 3 mm thick mild steel plate secured with 8 sets of bolts, a 2-HP diesel engine, and a pressure regulator with 1.4 - 14 kg/m2 capacity. The cap is placed over the stump of a pole, tree or bamboo and the preservative is forced into the wood with pressure from the engine.

Incising

First tested and patented by Kolossvary, Haltenberger, and Berdenich of Austria in 1911 and 1912 (U.S. pats. 1,012,207 and 1,018,624) with several improvements from O. P. M. Goss, D. W. Edwards and J. H. Mansfield among others, this process consists of making shallow, slit-like holes in the surfaces of material to be treated, so that deeper and more uniform penetration of preventative may be obtained. The term "incising" or perforating comes from Latin *incidere*, a compound of *in* and *caedere* (to cut). This process can also be used to ensure a long durability of food through its packaging. The air exchange can be ensured with laser-incised holes within packaging that are so fine that moisture does not escape. Incisions made in sawed material usually are parallel with the grain of the wood. This process is common in North America (since the 1950s), where Douglas-Fir products and pole butts of various species are prepared before treatment. It is most useful for woods that are resistant to side penetration but allow preservative transport along the grain. In the region in which it is produced, it is common practice to incise all sawed Douglas fir 3 in. or more in thickness before treatment.

Unfortunately the impregnation of Spruce, the most important structural timber large areas in Europe has shown that unsatisfactory treatment depths have been achieved with impregnation. The maximum penetration of 2 mm (1/12 in.) is not sufficient to protect wood in weathered positions. The present-day incising machines consist essentially of four revolving drums fitted with teeth or needles or with lasers that burn the incisions into the wood. Preservatives can be spread along the grain up to 20 mm (5/6 in.) in radial and up to 2 mm in (1/12 in.) tangential and radial direction.

In North America, where smaller timber dimensions are common, incision depths of 4 to 6 mm (1/6 to 1/4 in.) have become standard. In Europe, where larger dimensions are widespread, incision depths of 10 to 12 mm (1/2 in.) are necessary. The incisions are visible and often considered to be wood error. Incisions by laser are significantly smaller than those of spokes or needles. The costs for each process type are approximately for spoke/conventional all-round incising:

- 0.50 per m^2, by laser incising;
- 3.60 per m^2 and by needle incision; and
- 1.00 per m^2. .

Microwaving

An alternative method of increasing the permeability of timber involves using microwave technology. Ongoing research in this area is being conducted by the Cooperative Research Centre at the University of Melbourne, Australia.

LUMBER

Lumber or timber Wood on. Timber often refers to the wood contents of standing, live trees that can be used for lumber or fiber production, although it can also be used to describe sawn lumber whose smallest dimension is not less than 5 inches (127 mm).

Lumber is supplied either rough or finished. Besides pulpwood, *rough lumber* is the raw material for furniture-making and other items requiring additional cutting and shaping. It is available in many species, usually hardwoods. *Finished lumber* is supplied in standard sizes, mostly for the construction industry, primarily softwood from coniferous species including pine, cedar, hemlock, fir and spruce, but also some hardwood for high-grade flooring.

Terminology

In the United Kingdom and Australia, "timber" is a term also used for sawn wood products (that is, boards), whereas generally in the United States and Canada, the product of timber cut into boards is referred to as lumber. In the United States and Canada sawn wood products of five inches (127 mm) (nominal size) diameter or greater are sometimes called "timbers".

Dimensional Lumber

Dimensional lumber is a term used for lumber that is finished/planed and cut to standardized width and depth specified in inches. Examples of common sizes are 2 × 4 (also two-by-four and other variants such as four-b'-two in England, Australia, New Zealand), 2 × 6, and 4 × 4. The length of a board is usually specified separately from the width and depth. It is thus possible to find 2 × 4s that are four, eight, or twelve feet in length. In the United States the standard lengths of lumber are 6, 8, 10, 12, 14, 16, 18, 20, 22, and 24 feet.

Solid dimensional lumber typically is only available up to lengths of 24 ft, yet since builders have a need for lengths beyond that for roof construction (rafters), builders use "finger-jointed" lumber that can be up to 36 ft long in 2 × 6 size (see Engineered Lumber below). Finger-jointed lumber is also widely used for smaller lengths like studs, the vertical members of a framed wall. Pre-cut studs save a framer a lot of time as they are pre-cut by the manufacturer to be used in 8 ft, 9 ft and 10 ft ceiling applications, which means they have removed a few inches of the piece to allow for the sill plate and the double top plate with no additional sizing necessary by the framer.

In the Americas, *two-bys* (2 × 4s, 2 × 6s, 2 × 8s, 2 × 10s, and 2 × 12s), along with the 4 × 4, are common lumber sizes used in modern construction. They are the basic building block for such common structures as balloon-frame or platform-frame housing. Dimensional lumber made from softwood is typically used for construction, while hardwood boards are more commonly used for making cabinets or furniture.

The nominal size of a board varies from the actual size of the board. This is due to planing and shrinkage as the board is dried. This results in the final lumber being slightly smaller than the nominal size. Also, if the wood is surfaced when it is green, the initial dimensions are slightly larger. As the wood dries, it shrinks and reaches the specified actual dimensions.

In North America sizes for dimensional lumber made from hardwoods varies from the sizes for softwoods. Boards are usually supplied in random widths and lengths of a specified thickness, and sold by the board-foot (144 cubic inches, 1/12th of a cubic foot). This does not apply in all countries, for example in Australia many boards are sold to timber yards in packs with a common profile (dimensions) but not necessarily of consisting of the same length boards. Hardwoods cut for furniture are cut in the fall and winter, after the sap has stopped running in the trees. If hardwoods are cut in the spring or summer the sap ruins the natural color of the timber and deteriorates the value of the timber for furniture.

Also in North America hardwood lumber is commonly sold in a "quarter" system when referring to thickness. 4/4 (four quarters) refers to a one-inch thick board, 8/4 (eight quarters) is a two-inch thick board, etc. This system is not usually used for softwood lumber, although softwood decking is sometimes sold as 5/4 (actually one inch thick).

Engineered Lumber

Engineered lumber is lumber created by a manufacturer and designed for a certain structural purpose. The main categories of engineered lumber are:

- *Laminated Veneer Lumber (LVL)* – LVL comes in 1+3/4 inch thicknesses with depths such as 9+1/2, 11+7/8, 13, 16, 18, or 24 inches, and are typically doubled or tripled up. They function as beams to provide support over large spans, such as removed support walls and garage door openings, places where dimensional lumber isn't structurally sound to use, and also in areas where a heavy load is bearing from a floor, wall or roof above on a somewhat short span where dimensional lumber isn't practical. This type of lumber cannot be altered by holes or notches anywhere within the span or at the ends, as it compromises the integrity of the beam, but nails can be driven into it wherever necessary to anchor the beam or to add hangers for I-joists or dimensional lumber joists that terminate at an LVL beam.

- *Wood I-joists* – Sometimes called "TJI®" or "Trus Joists®", both of which are brands of wood I-joists, they are used for floor joists on upper floors and also in first floor conventional foundation construction on piers as opposed to slab floor construction. They are engineered for long spans and are doubled up in places where a wall will be placed over them, and sometimes tripled where heavy roof-loaded support walls are placed above them. They consist of a top and bottom chord/flange made from LVL with a webbing in-between made from oriented strand board (OSB). The webbing can be removed up to certain sizes/ shapes according to the manufacturer's or engineer's specifications, but for small holes, wood I-joists come with "knockouts", which are perforated, precut areas where holes can be made easily, typically without engineering approval. When large holes are needed, they can typically be made in the webbing only and only in the center third of the span; the top and bottom chords cannot be cut. Sizes and shapes of the hole, and typically the placing of a hole itself, must be approved by an engineer prior to the cutting of the hole and in many areas, a sheet showing the calculations made by the engineer must be provided to the building inspection authorities before the hole will be approved. Some I-joists are made with W-style webbing like a truss to eliminate cutting and allow ductwork to pass through.

- *Finger-Jointed Lumber* – Solid dimensional lumber lengths typically are limited to lengths of 22 to 24 feet, but can be made longer by the technique of "finger-jointing" lumber by using small solid pieces, usually 18 to 24 inches long, and joining them together using finger joints and glu to produce lengths that can be up to 36 feet long in 2×6 size. Finger-jointing also is predominant in precut wall studs.

- *Glu-lam Beams* – Created from 2×4 or 2×6 stock by gluing thefaces together to create beams such as 4×12 or 6×16. LVL beams have taken their place in most home construction. Manufactured Trusses – Trusses are used in home construction as bracing to support the roof rafters in the attic space. It is seen as an easier installation and a better solution for supporting roofs as opposed to the use of dimensional lumber's struts and purlins as bracing. In the southern USA and other parts, stick-framing with dimensional lumber roof support is still predominant. The main drawback of trusses is that less attic space is usable. Likewise they do lower labour times and cost.
- *Oriented Strand Board (OSB)* – OSB is made by laminating large, thin wood chips with glue, such that the grain orientation of the chips is random, making the OSB panels equally stiff in all directions. OSB has replaced plywood for use as exterior wall sheathing and roof decking (7/16 inch minimum thickness) and in second-story flooring (3/4 inch thickness in a tongue-and-groove interlocking pattern), which is nailed and glued to the I-joists. OSB used in wall sheathing and roof decking will swell if exposed to the elements for even a brief time and must be replaced; therefore, it is covered by a weatherproof membrane such as felt or spun-bonded olefin (Tyvek®) to protect it, secured with plastic cap nails. House wrapping is used on areas which will be sheathed with vinyl siding. 3/4 inch tongue-and-groove OSB flooring is coated to protect it from the elements for a short time until the structure is roofed over. Moisture resistant OSB is often specified for use as a roof underlayment.

Defects in Lumber

Defects occurring in Timber are grouped into the following *five* divisions:

Defects due to Conversion

During the process of converting timber to commercial form, the following defects may occur:

- Chip mark
- Diagonal grain
- Torn grain
- Wane

Defects due to Fungi

- Fungi attacks timber when these conditions are all present:
- The timber moisture content is above 20%
- The environment is warm enough
- There is air

Wood with less than 20% moisture remains free of fungi for centuries. Similarly, wood submerged in water will not be attacked by fungi because of absence of air.

Fungi timber defects:

- Blue stain
- Brown rot
- Dry rot
- Heart rot
- Sap stain
- Wet rot
- White rot

Defects due to Insects

Following are the insects which are usually responsible for the decay of timber:

- Beetles
- Marine Borers

- Termites
- Red Ants

Defects due to Natural Forces

The main natural forces responsible for causing defects in timber are *two*, namely, *abnormal growth* and *rupture of tissues.*

Defects due to Seasoning

Defects due to seasoning are the number one cause for splinters and slivers.

Preservatives

Fasteners used with treated lumber require special consideration because of the corrosive chemicals used in the treatment process.

Timber or lumber may be treated with a preservative that protects it from being destroyed by insects, fungus or exposure to moisture. Generally this is applied through combined vacuum and pressure treatment. The preservatives used to pressure-treat lumber are classified as pesticides. Due to potential hazards to humans and the environment, some are being phased out. Many newer preservatives are free of metallic compounds altogether, and are instead based on biodegradable organic chemistry. Treating lumber provides long-term resistance to organisms that cause deterioration. If it is applied correctly, it extends the productive life of lumber by five to ten times. If left untreated, wood that is exposed to moisture or soil for sustained periods of time will become weakened by various types of fungi, bacteria or insects.

Timber Framing

Timber framing is a style of construction which uses heavier framing elements than modern *stick framing,* which uses dimensional lumber. The timbers originally were tree boles squared with a broadaxe or adze and joined together with joinery without nails. A modern imitation with sawn timbers is growing in popularity in the United States.

One of the most conventional framing methods is the *Neumann Notch*, which involves a 32 degree angling of adjoining lumber and then a right-angled wedge with an eighteen degree cusp fitted between the lumber before being bolted. This convention was pioneered by Daniel R. Neumann, a carpenter from Germany, that was responsible for the structural development of the Massachusetts Bay Colony in 1630. This framing convention spread to construction sites in other colonies, most famously Plymouth and Concord. Neumann's notched framing then was adopted by carpenters and construction companies and this framing convention is still used today in traditional frame sets.

Another somewhat less conventional method for framing is known as the "New-style" binding. The basic setup of the New-style binding was developed by Austin D. New, a Mormon settler in Salt Lake City, Utah during the 1800s. The basic structure of the New-style binding involves a set-up of two similar sized logs set against each other perpendicularly and lashed together with hemp rope. This technique was used to construct many of the early houses of the Mormon settlers due to its ease of use and durability. Eventually the New-style binding became obsolete as the settlers began constructing homes out of the more traditional brick and mortar.

Residual Wood

Coal-fired power plant in Pepeekeo, Hawaii, that formerly provided electricity to a sugar mill is now being converted into a 24-megawatt (MW) biomass power plant. MMA Renewable Ventures is financing the conversion and will operate the new plant, which will be called the Hu Honua Bioenergy Facility. Located about 8 miles north of Hilo on the Big Island of Hawaii, the facility will draw on residual wood from the local timber industry and other biomass wastes to produce enough power for about 18,000 homes, meeting up to 10% of the Big Island's electricity needs.

Wood Drying

For some purposes wood is not dried at all (it is used "*green*"). Often the wood needs to be in an equilibrium with the air outside (e.g. construction wood) or the air indoors (e.g. for furniture). Wood is either air-dried or kiln-dried. Usually the wood is sawn prior to the drying process, but not always (i.e. drying the whole log)

Types of Wood

Wood is divided, according to its botanical origin, into two kinds: Softwoods from coniferous trees and hardwoods from broadleaved trees. Structurally softwoods are generally simple in structure and lighter whereas hardwoods are generally complex in structure and harder.

Softwood (like pine wood) is much lighter and easier to process than the heavy hardwood (like fruit tree wood). The density of softwoods ranges between 350-700 kg/m^3, while hardwoods are 450-1250 kg/m^3. Both consist of approximately 12% moisture (*Desch and Dinwoodie, 1996*). Due to the more dense and complex structure of hardwood, the permeability is very low in comparison to softwood, thus making it more difficult to dry. Even though there are about hundred times more species of hardwood trees than softwood trees, the ability to process and dry softwood much more easy and faster makes it the main supply of commercial wood today.

Wood-water Relationships

The timber of living trees and freshly felled logs contains a large amount of water, which often constitutes more weight than the actual wood. Water has a significant influence on wood: wood continually exchanges moisture (water) with its surroundings, although the rate of exchange is strongly affected by the degree wood is sealed.

Water in wood may be present in two forms:

Free water: The bulk of water contained in the cell lumina is only held by capillary forces: it is not bound chemically and is termed free water. Free water is not in the same thermodynamic state as liquid water: energy is required to overcome the capillary forces. Furthermore, free water may contain chemicals, altering the drying characteristics.

Bound or hygroscopic water: Bound water is bound to the wood via hydrogen bonds. The attraction of wood for water arises from the presence of free hydroxyl (OH) groups in the cellulose, hemicelluloses and lignin molecules in the cell wall. The hydroxyl groups are negatively charged electrically. Water is a polar liquid. The free hydroxyl groups in cellulose attract and hold water by hydrogen bonding.

Water in cell lumina may be in the form of water vapour, but the total amount is normally negligible, at normal temperatures and moisture contents.

Moisture Content of Wood

The moisture content of wood is calculated by the formula mass (the attainment of constant mass generally after drying in an oven set at 103 +/- 2 °C for 24 hours as mentioned by Walker *et al.*, 1993). This can also be expressed as a fraction of the mass of the water and the mass of the oven-dry wood rather than a percentage, for example, 0.59 kg/kg (oven dry basis) expresses the same moisture content as 59% (oven dry basis).

Fibre Saturation Point

When green wood dries, the first water to go is the free water from the cell lumina. It is held only by the capillary forces. Most physical properties, such as strength and shrinkage, are unaffected by the removal of free water. The fibre saturation point (FSP) is defined as the moisture content at which free water should be completely gone, while the cell walls are saturated with bound water. In most woods, the fibre saturation point is at 25 to 30% moisture content. Siau (1984) reported that the fibre saturation point (kg/kg) is dependent on the temperature T (°C) according to the following equation:

Many important properties of wood show a considerable change as the wood is dried below the fibre saturation point. These include:

- *Volume:* ideally no shrinkage occurs until some bound water is lost, i.e. until the wood is dried below FSP.

- Most strength properties show a consistent increase as the wood is dried below the FSP (Desch and Dinwoodie, 1996). An exception is impact bending strength and, in some cases toughness.
- Electrical resistivity increases very rapidly with the loss of bound water when the wood dries below the FSP.

Equilibrium Moisture Content

Wood is a hygroscopic substance. It has the ability to take in or give off moisture in the form of vapour. The water contained in wood exerts a vapour pressure of its own, which is determined by the maximum size of the capillaries filled with water at any time. If the water vapour pressure in the ambient space is lower than the vapour pressure within wood, desorption takes place. The largest sized capillaries, which are full of water at the time, empty first. The vapour pressure within the wood falls as water is successively contained in smaller and smaller sized capillaries. A stage is eventually reached when the vapour pressure within the wood equals the vapour pressure in the ambient space above the wood, and further desorption ceases. The amount of moisture that remains in the wood at this stage is in equilibrium with the water vapour pressure in the ambient space, and is termed the equilibrium moisture content or EMC. Because of its hygroscopicity, wood tends to reach a moisture content that is in equilibrium with the relative humidity and temperature of the surrounding air. The EMC of wood varies with the ambient relative humidity (a function of temperature) significantly, to a lesser degree with the temperature. It is reported that the EMC also varies very slightly with species, mechanical stress, drying history of wood, density, extractives content and the direction of sorption in which the moisture change takes place (i.e. adsorption or desorption).

Moisture Content of Wood in Service

Wood retains its hygroscopic characteristics after it is put into use. It is then subjected to fluctuating humidity, the dominant factor in determining its EMC. These fluctuations may be more or less cyclical, such as diurnal changes or annual seasonal changes. In order to minimise the changes in wood moisture content or the movement of wooden objects in service, wood is usually dried to a moisture content that is close to the average EMC conditions to which it will be exposed. These conditions vary for interior uses compared with exterior uses in a given geographic location. For example, according to the Australian Standard for Timber Drying Quality (AS/NZS 4787, 2001), the EMC is recommended to be 10-12% for the majority of Australian states, although extreme cases may be up to 15 to 18% for some places in Queensland, Northern Territory, Western Australia and Tasmania. However, the EMC may be as low as 6 to 7% in dry centrally heated houses and offices or in permanently air-conditioned buildings.

The primary reason for drying wood to a moisture content equivalent to its mean EMC under use conditions is to minimise the dimensional changes (or movement) in the final product.

Shrinkage and Swelling

Shrinkage and swelling may occur in wood when the moisture content is changed (Stamm, 1964). Shrinkage occurs as moisture content decreases, while swelling takes place when it increases. Volume change is not equal in all directions. The greatest dimensional change occurs in a direction tangential to the growth rings. Shrinkage from the pith outwards, or radially, is usually considerably less than tangential shrinkage, while longitudinal (along the grain) shrinkage is so slight as to be usually neglected. The longitudinal shrinkage is 0.1 to 0.3%, in contrast to transverse shrinkages, which is 2-10%. Tangential shrinkage is often about twice as great as in the radial direction, although in some species it may be as much as five times as great. The shrinkage is about 5 to 10% in the tangential direction and about 2 to 6% in the radial direction.

WOOD DRYING

Wood drying may be described as the art of ensuring that gross dimensional changes through shrinkage are confined to the drying process. Ideally, wood is dried to that equilibrium moisture content as will later (in service) be attained by the wood. Thus, further dimensional change will be kept to a minimum.

It is probably impossible to completely eliminate movement in wood, but this may be approximated by chemical modification. This is the treatment of wood with chemicals to replace the hydroxyl groups with other hydrophobic functional groups of modifying agents. Among all the existing processes, wood modification with acetic anhydride has considerable promise due to the high anti-shrink or anti-swell efficiency (ASE) attainable without damaging the wood properties. However, acetylation of wood has been slow to be commercialised due to the cost, corrosion and the entrapment of the acetic acid in wood. There is extensive literature relating to the chemical modification of wood.

Drying timber is one approach for adding value to sawn products from the primary wood processing industries. According to the Australian Forest and Wood Products Research and Development Corporation (FWPRDC), green sawn hardwood, which is sold at about $350 per cubic metre or less, increases in value to $2,000 per cubic metre or more with drying and processing. However, currently-used conventional drying processes often result in significant quality problems from cracks, both externally and internally, reducing the value of the product. As an example, in Queensland alone, assuming that 10% of the dried softwood is devalued by $200 per cubic metre because of drying defects, sawmillers are losing about $5 million per year in that State alone. Australia wide this could be $40 million per year for softwood and an equal or higher amount for hardwood. Thus proper drying under controlled conditions (prior to use) is of great importance in timber utilisation in any country, where climatic conditions vary considerably at different times of the year.

Drying, if carried out promptly after the felling of trees, also protects timber against primary decay, fungal stain and attack by certain kinds of insects. Organisms, which cause decay and stain, generally cannot thrive in timber with a moisture content below 20%. Several, though not all, insect pests can live only in green timber. Dried wood is less susceptible to decay than green wood (above 20% moisture content).

Apart from the above important advantages of drying timber, the following points are also significant:

- Dried timber is lighter, and hence the transportation and handling costs are reduced.
- Dried timber is stronger than green timber in most strength properties.
- Timbers for impregnation with preservatives have to be properly dried if proper penetration is to be accomplished, particularly in the case of oil-type preservatives.
- In the field of chemical modification of wood and wood products, the material should be dried to a certain moisture content for the appropriate reactions to occur.
- Dry wood works, machines, finishes and glues better than green timber. Paints and finishes last longer on dry timber.
- The electrical and thermal insulation properties of wood are improved by drying.

Prompt drying of wood immediately after felling therefore results in significant upgrading of, and value adding to, the raw timber. Drying enables substantial long term economy in timber utilisation by rationalising the utilisation of timber resources. The drying of wood is thus an area for research and development, which concerns many researchers and timber companies around the world.

How Wood Dries: The Mechanisms of Moisture Movement

Water in wood normally moves from zones of higher to zones of lower moisture content (Walker *et al.*, 1993). In simple terms, this means that drying starts from the outside and moves towards the centre, and it also means that drying at the outside is also necessary to expel moisture from the inner zones of the wood. Wood, after a period of time, attains a moisture content in equilibrium with the surrounding air (the EMC, as mentioned earlier).

Mechanisms for Moisture Movement

The basic driving force for moisture movement is chemical potential. However, it is not always straightforward to relate chemical potential in wood to commonly observable variables, such as temperature and moisture content. Moisture in wood moves within the wood as liquid or vapour through several types of passageways depending on the nature of the driving force, (e.g. pressure or moisture gradient), and variations in wood structure, as explained in the next section on driving forces for moisture movement. These pathways consist of cavities of the vessels, fibres, ray cells, pit chambers and their pit membrane openings, intercellular spaces and transitory cell wall passageways. Movement of water takes place in these passageways in any direction, longitudinally in the cells, as well as laterally from cell to cell until it reaches the lateral drying surfaces of the wood. The higher longitudinal permeability of sapwood of hardwood is generally caused by the presence of vessels. The lateral permeability and transverse flow is often very low in hardwoods. The vessels in hardwoods are sometimes blocked by the presence of tyloses and/or by secreting gums and resins in some other species, as mentioned earlier. The presence of gum veins, the formation of which is often a result of natural protective response of trees to injury, is commonly observed on the surface of sawn boards of most eucalypts. Despite the generally higher volume fraction of rays in hardwoods (typically 15% of wood volume), the rays are not particularly effective in radial flow, nor are the pits on the radial surfaces of fibres effective in tangential flow.

Moisture Movement Space

The available space for air and moisture in wood depends on the density and porosity of wood. Porosity is the volume fraction of void space in a solid. The porosity is reported to be 1.2 to 4.6% of dry volume of wood cell wall (Siau, 1984). On the other hand, permeability is a measure of the ease with which fluids are transported through a porous solid under the influence of some driving forces, e.g. capillary pressure gradient or moisture gradient. It is clear that solids must be porous to be permeable, but it does not necessarily follow that all porous bodies are permeable. Permeability can only exist if the void spaces are interconnected by openings. For example, a hardwood may be permeable because there is intervessel pitting with openings in the membranes. If these membranes are occluded or encrusted, or if the pits are aspirated, the wood assumes a closed-cell structure and may be virtually impermeable. The density is also important for impermeable hardwoods because more cell-wall material is traversed per unit distance, which offers increased resistance to diffusion. Hence lighter woods, in general, dry more rapidly than do the heavier woods. The transport of fluids is often bulk flow (momentum transfer) for permeable softwoods at high temperature while diffusion occurs for impermeable hardwoods (Siau, 1984). These mechanisms are discussed below.

Driving Forces for Moisture Movement

Three main driving forces used in different version of diffusion models are moisture content, the partial pressure of water vapour, and the chemical potential. These are discussed here, including capillary action, which is a mechanism for free water transport in permeable softwoods. Total pressure difference is the driving force during wood vacuum drying.

Capillary Action

Capillary forces determine the movements (or absence of movement) of free water. It is due to both adhesion and cohesion. Adhesion is the attraction between water to other substances and cohesion is the attraction of the molecules in water to each other.

As wood dries, evaporation of water from the surface sets up capillary forces that exert a pull on the free water in the zones of wood beneath the surfaces. When there is no longer any free water in the wood capillary forces are no longer of importance.

Moisture Content Differences

The chemical potential is explained here since it is the true driving force for the transport of water in both liquid and vapour phases in wood. The Gibbs free energy per mole of substance is usually expressed as the chemical potential. The chemical potential of unsaturated air or wood below the fibre saturation point influences the drying of wood. Equilibrium will occur at the equilibrium moisture content (as defined earlier) of wood when the chemical potential of the wood becomes equal to that of the surrounding air. The chemical potential of sorbed water is a function of wood moisture content. Therefore, a gradient of wood moisture content (between surface and centre), or more specifically of activity, is accompanied by a gradient of chemical potential under isothermal conditions. Moisture will redistribute itself throughout the wood until the chemical potential is uniform throughout, resulting in a zero potential gradient at equilibrium. The flux of moisture attempting to achieve the equilibrium state is assumed to be proportional to the difference in chemical potential, and inversely proportional to the path length over which the potential difference acts.

The gradient in chemical potential is related to the moisture content gradient as explained in above equations. The diffusion model using moisture content gradient as a driving force was applied successfully. Though the agreement between the moisture-content profiles predicted by the diffusion model based on moisture-content gradients is better at lower moisture contents than at higher ones, there is no evidence to suggest that there are significantly different moisture-transport mechanisms operating at higher moisture contents for this timber. Their observations are consistent with a transport process that is driven by the total concentration of water. The diffusion model is used for this thesis based on this empirical evidence that the moisture-content gradient is a driving force for drying this type of impermeable timber.

Differences in moisture content between the surface and the centre (gradient, the chemical potential difference between interface and bulk) move the bound water through the small passageways in the cell wall by diffusion. In comparison with capillary movement, diffusion is a slow process. Diffusion is the generally suggested mechanism for the drying of impermeable hardwoods. Furthermore, moisture migrates slowly due to the fact that extractives plug the small cell wall openings in the heartwood. This is why sapwood generally dries faster than heartwood under the same drying conditions.

Moisture Movement Directions for Diffusion

It is reported that the ratio of the longitudinal to the transverse (radial and tangential) diffusion rates for wood ranges from about 100 at a moisture content of 5% to 2 to 4 at a moisture content of 25%. Radial diffusion is somewhat faster than tangential diffusion. Although longitudinal diffusion is most rapid, it is of practical importance only when short pieces are dried. Generally the timber boards are much longer than in width or thickness. For example, a typical size of a green board used for this research was 6 m long, 250 mm in width and 43 mm in thickness. If the boards are quartersawn (sawing around the pith), then the width will be in the radial direction whereas the thickness will be in tangential direction, and *vice versa* for back-sawn (sawing through and through) boards. Most of the moisture is removed from wood by lateral movement during drying.

Reasons for Splits and Cracks during Timber Drying and their Control

The chief difficulty experienced in the drying of timber is the tendency of its outer layers to dry out more rapidly than the interior ones. If these layers are allowed to dry much below the fibre saturation point while the interior is still saturated, stresses (called drying stresses) are set up because the shrinkage of the outer layers is restricted by the wet interior. Rupture in the wood tissues occurs, and consequently splits and cracks occur if these stresses across the grain exceed the strength across the grain (fibre to fibre bonding).

The successful control of drying defects in a drying process consists in maintaining a balance between the rate of evaporation of moisture from the surface and the rate of outward movement of moisture from the interior of the wood. The way in which drying can be controlled will now be explained.

Influence of Temperature, Relative Humidity and Rate of Air Circulation

The external drying conditions (temperature, relative humidity and air velocity) control the external boundary conditions for drying, and hence the drying rate, as well as affecting the rate of internal moisture movement. The drying rate is affected by external drying conditions as will now be described.

Temperature: If the relative humidity is kept constant, the higher the temperature, the higher the drying rate. Temperature influences the drying rate by increasing the moisture holding capacity of the air, as well as by accelerating the diffusion rate of moisture through the wood. The actual temperature in a drying kiln is the dry-bulb temperature (usually denoted by Tg), which is the temperature of a vapour-gas mixture determined by inserting a thermometer with a dry bulb. On the other hand, the wet-bulb temperature (TW) is defined as the temperature reached by a small amount of liquid evaporating in a large amount of an unsaturated air-vapour mixture. The temperature sensing element of this thermometer is kept moist with a porous fabric sleeve (cloth) usually put in a reservoir of clean water. A minimum air flow of 2 m/s is needed to prevent a zone of stagnant damp air formation around the sleeve. Since air passes over the wet sleeve, water is evaporated and cools the wet-bulb thermometer. The difference between the dry-bulb and wet-bulb temperatures, the wet-bulb depression, is used to determine the relative humidity from a standard hygrometric chart. A higher difference between the dry-bulb and wet-bulb temperatures indicates a lower relative humidity. For example, if the dry-bulb temperature is 100 °C and wet-bulb temperature 60 °C, then the relative humidity is read as 17% from a hygrometric chart.

Relative humidity: The relative humidity of air is defined as the partial pressure of water vapour divided by the saturated vapour pressure at the same temperature and total pressure. If the temperature is kept constant, lower relative humidities result in higher drying rates due to the increased moisture gradient in wood, resulting from the reduction of the moisture content in the surface layers when the relative humidity of air is reduced. The relative humidity is usually expressed on a percentage basis. For drying, the other essential parameter related to relative humidity is the absolute humidity, which is the mass of water vapour per unit mass of dry air (kg of water per kg of dry air). The following equation can be used to calculate the absolute humidity from the relative humidity.

Air circulation rate: Drying time and timber quality depend on the air velocity and its uniform circulation. At a constant temperature and relative humidity, the highest possible drying rate is obtained by rapid circulation of air across the surface of wood, giving rapid removal of moisture evaporating from the wood. However, a higher drying rate is not always desirable, particularly for impermeable hardwoods, because higher drying rates develop greater stresses that may cause the timber to crack or distort. At very low fan speeds, less than 1 m s-1, the air flow through the stack is often laminar flow, and the heat transfer between the timber surface and the moving air stream is not particularly effective The low effectiveness (externally) of heat transfer is not necessarily a problem if internal moisture movement is the key limitation to the movement of moisture, as it is for most hardwoods.

Classification of Timbers for Drying

The timbers are classified as follows according to their ease of drying and their proneness to drying degrade:

(a) Highly refractory woods: These woods are slow and difficult to dry if the final product is to be free from defects, particularly cracks and splits. Examples are heavy structural timbers with high density such as ironbark (*Eucalyptus paniculata*), blackbutt (*E. pilularis*), southern blue gum (*E. globulus*) and brush box (*Lophostemon cofertus*). They require considerable protection and care against rapid drying conditions for the best results.

(b) Moderately refractory woods: These timbers show a moderate tendency to crack and split during seasoning. They can be seasoned free from defects with moderately rapid drying conditions (i.e. a maximum dry-bulb temperature of 85 °C can be used). Examples are Sydney blue gum (*E. saligna*) and other timbers of medium density (Bootle, 1994), which are potentially suitable for furniture.

(c) Non-refractory woods: These woods can be rapidly seasoned to be free from defects even by applying high temperatures (dry-bulb temperatures of more than 100 °C) in industrial kilns. If not dried rapidly, they may develop discolouration (blue stain) and mould on the surface. Examples are softwoods and low density timbers such as *Pinus radiata*.

Methods of Drying Timber

Broadly, there are two methods by which timber can be dried: (i) natural drying or air drying, and (ii) artificial drying.

Air Drying

Air drying is the drying of timber by exposing it to the air. The technique of air drying consists mainly of making a stack of sawn timber (with the layers of boards separated by stickers) on raised foundations, in a clean, cool, dry and shady place. Rate of drying largely depends on climatic conditions, and on the air movement (exposure to the wind). For successful air drying, a continuous and uniform flow of air throughout the pile of the timber needs to be arranged (Desch and Dinwoodie, 1996). The rate of loss of moisture can be controlled by coating the planks with any substance that is relatively impermeable to moisture; ordinary mineral oil is usually quite effective. Coating the ends of logs with oil or thick paint, improves their quality upon drying. Wrapping planks or logs in materials which will allow some movement of moisture, generally works very well provided the wood is first treated against fungal infection by coating in petrol/gasoline or oil. Mineral oil will generally not soak in more than 1-2 mm below the surface and is easily removed by planing when the timber is suitably dry.

Kiln Drying

The process of kiln drying consists basically of introducing heat. This may be directly, using natural gas and/or electricity or indirectly, through steam-heated heat exchangers, although solar energy is also possible. In the process, deliberate control of temperature, relative humidity and air circulation is provided to give conditions at various stages (moisture contents or times) of drying the timber to achieve effective drying. For this purpose, the timber is stacked in chambers, called wood drying kilns, which are fitted with equipment for manipulation and control of the temperature and the relative humidity of the drying air and its circulation rate through the timber stack (Walker *et al.*, 1993; Desch and Dinwoodie, 1996).

Kiln drying provides a means of overcoming the limitations imposed by erratic weather conditions. In kiln drying as in air drying, unsaturated air is used as the drying medium. Almost all commercial timbers of the world are dried in industrial kilns. A comparison of air drying, conventional kiln and solar drying is given below:

- Timber can be dried to any desired low moisture content by conventional or solar kiln drying, but in air drying, moisture contents of less than 18% are difficult to attain for most locations.
- The drying times are considerably less in conventional kiln drying than in solar kiln drying, followed by air drying.
- This means that if capital outlay is involved, this capital is just sitting there for a longer time when air drying is used. On the other hand, installing an industrial kiln, to say nothing of maintenance and operation, is expensive.
- In addition, wood that is being air dried takes up space, which could also cost money.
- In air drying, there is little control over the drying elements, so drying degrade cannot be controlled.
- The temperatures employed in kiln drying typically kill all the fungi and insects in the wood if a maximum dry-bulb temperature of above 60 °C is used for the drying schedule. This is not guaranteed in air drying.

If air drying is done improperly (exposed to the sun), the rate of drying may be overly rapid in the dry summer months, causing cracking and splitting, and too slow during the cold winter months.

The significant advantages of conventional kiln drying include higher throughput and better control of the final moisture content. Conventional kiln and solar drying both enable wood to be dried to any moisture content regardless of weather conditions. For most large-scale drying operations solar and conventional kiln drying are more efficient than air drying.

Compartment-type kilns are most commonly used in timber companies. A compartment kiln is filled with a static batch of timber through which air is circulated. In these types of kiln, the timber remains stationary. The drying conditions are successively varied from time to time in such a way that the kilns provide control over the entire charge of timber being dried. This drying method is well suited to the needs of timber companies, which have to dry timbers of varied species and thickness, including refractory hardwoods that are more liable than other species to check and split.

The main elements of kiln drying are described below:

(a) ***Construction materials:*** The kiln chambers are generally built of brick masonry, or hollow cement-concrete slabs. Sheet metal or prefabricated aluminium in a double-walled construction with sandwiched thermal insulation, such as glass wool or polyurethane foams, are materials that are also used in some modern kilns. Some of the elements used in kiln construction. However, brick masonry chambers, with lime and (mortar) plaster on the inside and painted with impermeable coatings, are used widely and have been found to be satisfactory for many applications.

(b) ***Heating:*** Heating is usually carried out by steam heat exchangers and pipes of various configurations (e.g. plain, or finned (transverse or longitudinal) tubes) or by large flue pipes through which hot gases from a wood burning furnace are passed. Only occasionally is electricity or gas employed for heating.

(c) ***Humidification:*** Humidification is commonly accomplished by introducing live steam into the kiln through a steam spray pipe. In order to limit and control the humidity of the air when large quantities of moisture are being rapidly evaporated from the timber, there is normally a provision for ventilation of the chamber in all types of kilns.

(d) *Air circulation:* Air circulation is the means for carrying the heat to and the moisture away from all parts of a load. Forced circulation kilns are most common, where the air is circulated by means of fans or blowers, which may be installed outside the kiln chamber (external fan kiln) or inside it (internal fan kiln). Throughout the process, it is necessary to keep close control of the moisture content using a moisture meter system in order to reduce over-drying and allow operators to know when to pull the charge Preferably, this in-kiln moisture meter will have an auto-shutoff feature.

Kiln Drying Schedules

Satisfactory kiln drying can usually be accomplished by regulating the temperature and humidity of the circulating air to suit the state of the timber at any given time. This condition is achieved by applying kiln-drying schedules. The desired objective of an appropriate schedule is to ensure drying timber at the fastest possible rate without causing objectionable degrade. The following factors have a considerable bearing on the schedules.

- The species; because of the variations in physical, mechanical and transport properties between species.
- The thickness of the timber; because the drying time is approximately inversely related to thickness and, to some extent, is also influenced by the width of the timber.
- Whether the timber boards are quarter-sawn, back-sawn or mixed-sawn; because sawing pattern influences the distortion due to shrinkage anisotropy.
- Permissible drying degrade; because aggressive drying schedules can cause timber to crack and distort.
- Intended use of timber; because the required appearance of the timber surface and the target final moisture contents are different depending on the uses of timber.

Considering each of the factors, no one schedule is necessarily appropriate, even for similar loads of the same species. This is why there is so much timber drying research, including this work, focused on the development of effective drying schedules.

Drying Defects

Drying defects are the most common form of degrade in timber, next to natural problems such as knots. There are two broad categories of drying defects (some defects involve both causes):

- defects that arise due to the shrinkage anisotropy. This leads to warping: cupping, bowing, twisting, spring and diamonding.
- defects that arise due to uneven drying. This leads to the rupture of the wood tissue: checks (surface, end and internal), end splits, honey-combing and case-hardening. Another such defect is collapse, often seen as a corrugation, or "washboarding" of the wood surface. Collapse is a defect that results from the physical flattening of fibres, above the fibre saturation point (thus not a form of shrinkage anisotropy).

Australian and New Zealand Standard Organisations (AS/ NZS 4787, 2001) have developed a standard for timber quality. Their five criteria for measuring drying quality:

- moisture content gradient and presence of residual drying stress (case-hardening);
- surface, internal and end checks;
- collapse;
- distortions; and
- discolouration caused by drying.

This standard also indicates how to assess each of these drying quality criteria and provides a classification to express drying quality.

CHAPTER 9

Fruit Tree

INTRODUCTION

A fruit tree is a tree bearing fruit — the structures formed by the ripened ovary of a flower containing one or more seeds. However, because all trees of flowering plants produce fruit (essentially all trees except tree ferns and gymnosperms), the term in horticultural usage applies to trees providing fruit as human food. Types of fruits are described and defined elsewhere (see Fruit), but would include *fruit* in a culinary sense as well as some nut bearing trees, like walnuts.

The scientific study and the cultivation of fruits is called pomology, which divides up fruits into groups based on plant morphology and anatomy. Some of those groups are: Pome fruits, which include apples and pears. And stone fruits which include peaches/nectarines, almonds, apricots, plums and cherries

Examples of Tree Fruit

- Apple
- Almond
- Amla (Indian Gooseberry)
- Apricot
- Avocado
- (Ber)

- Bael
- Banana
- Cashew
- Cherry
- Citrus (Orange, Lemon, Lime, etc.)
- Coconut
- Durian
- Guava
- Jujube
- Jackfruit
- Lychee
- Mango
- Medlar
- Morello cherry
- Olive
- Pawpaw
- Pear
- Peach and Nectarine
- Persimmon
- Plum
- Pomegranate
- Sapodilla (Chikoo)
- Sugar-apple (Sharifa)
- Tamarillo
- Walnut

List of Culinary Fruits

This list of culinary fruits contains the names of some fruits that are considered edible in some cuisines. The definition of fruit for these lists is a culinary fruit, i.e. "Any sweet, edible part of a plant that resembles fruit, even if it does not develop from a floral ovary; also used in a technically imprecise sense for some sweet or sweetish vegetables, some of which may resemble a true fruit or are used in cookery as if they were a fruit, for example rhubarb.

Note that many items that are *true fruits* botanically speaking, are not considered culinary fruits. They are classified as vegetables in the culinary sense, (for example: the tomato, cucumber, zucchini, and so on), and hence they do not appear in this list. There also exist many fruits which are edible and palatable but for various reasons have not become popular.

TEMPERATE FRUITS

Fruits of temperate climates are almost always borne on trees or woody shrubs or lianas. They will not grow adequately in the tropics, as they need a period of cold (a chilling requirement) each year before they will flower. The apple, pear, cherry, and plum are the most widely grown and eaten, owing to their adaptability. Many other fruits are important regionally but do not figure prominently in commerce. Many sorts of small fruit on this list are gathered from the wild, just as they were in Neolithic times.

Rosaceae Family

The family Rosaceae dominates the temperate fruits, both in numbers and in importance. The pome fruits, stone fruits and brambles are fruits of plants in Rosaceae.

The pome fruits:

Apples

- Apple and crabapple (*Malus*)
- Chokeberry (*Aronia*)
- Hawthorn (*Crataegus* and *Rhaphiolepis*)
- Loquat (*Eryobotrya japonica*)
- Medlar (*Mespilus germanica*)
- Pear, European and Asian species (*Pyrus*)

- Quince (*Cydonia oblonga* and *Chaenomeles*)
- Rose hip, the fruitlike base of roses (*Rosa*); used mostly for jams and herbal tea
- Rowan (*Sorbus*)
- Service tree (*Sorbus domestica*), bears a fruit known as a sorb or sorb apple
- Serviceberry or Saskatoon (*Amelanchier*)
- Shipova (× *Sorbopyrus auricularis*)

The stone fruits, drupes of genus *Prunus*:

- Apricot (*Prunus armeniaca* or *Armeniaca vulgaris*)
- Cherry, sweet, black, sour, and wild species (*Prunus avium*, *Prunus serotina*, *P. cerasus*, and others)
- Chokecherry (*Prunus virginiana*)
- Greengage, a cultivar of the plum
- Hybrids of the preceding species, such as the pluot, aprium and peacotum
- Peach (of the normal and white variety) and its variant the nectarine (*Prunus persica*)
- Plum, of which there are several domestic and wild species; dried plums are called prunes

Berries

In non-technical usage, berry means any small fruit that can be eaten whole and lacks objectionable seeds. The bramble fruits, compound fruits of genus *Rubus* (blackberries), are some of the most popular pseudo-berries:

Raspberries

- Blackberry, of which there are many species and hybrids, such as dewberry, boysenberry, olallieberry, and tayberry (genus *Rubus*)
- Cloudberry (*Rubus chamaemorus*)

- Loganberry (*Rubus loganobaccus*)
- Raspberry, several species (genus *Rubus*)
- Salmonberry (*Rubus spectabilis*)
- Thimbleberry (*Rubus parviflorus*)
- Wineberry (*Rubus phoenicolasius*)

The true berries are dominated by the family Ericaceae, many of which are hardy in the subarctic:

- Bearberry (*Arctostaphylos* spp.)
- Bilberry or whortleberry (*Vaccinium* spp.)
- Blueberry (*Vaccinium* spp.)
- Crowberry (*Empetrum* spp.)
- Cranberry (*Vaccinium* spp.)
- Huckleberry (*Vaccinium* spp.)
- Lingonberry (*Vaccinium vitis-idaea*)
- Strawberry Tree (*Arbutus unedo*), not to be confused with the Strawberry (*Fragaria*)

Other berries not in the Rosaceae or Ericaceae:

- Açaí (*Euterpe*), a palm fruit native to the Amazon region
- Barberry (*Berberis*; Berberidaceae)
- Currant (*Ribes* spp.; Grossulariaceae), red, black, and white types
- Eggplant (*Solanum melongena* Solanaceae), purple berry thought to be a vegetable
- Elderberry (*Sambucus*; Caprifoliaceae)
- Gooseberry (*Ribes* spp.; Grossulariaceae)
- Hackberry (*Celtis* spp.; Cannabaceae)
- Honeysuckle: the berries of *some* species (called honeyberries) are edible, others are poisonous (*Lonicera* spp.; Caprifoliaceae)

- Mulberry (*Morus* spp.; Moraceae) including:
- Red Mulberry (*Morus rubra*)
- White Mulberry (*Morus alba*)
- Mayapple (*Podophyllum* spp.; Berberidaceae)
- Nannyberry or sheepberry (*Viburnum* spp.; Caprifoliaceae)
- Oregon grape (*Mahonia aquifolium*; Berberidaceae)
- Sea-buckthorn (*Hippophae rhamnoides*; Elaeagnaceae)
- Sea Grape (*Coccoloba uvifera*; Polygonaceae)
- Tomato (*Solanum lycopersicum* Solanaceae), a red juicy berry thought to be a vegetable as served in salads.
- Wolfberry (*Lycium barbarum, Lycium* spp.; Solanaceae)

FRUITS OF ASIAN ORIGIN

Some fruits native to Asia or of Asian Origin.

- Arhat (*Siraitia grosvenorii*; Cucurbitaceae) Also called longevity fruit
- Coconut (*Cocos* spp.; Arecaceae)
- Che (*Cudrania tricuspidata*; Moraceae) Also called Cudrania, Chinese Mulberry, Cudrang, Mandarin Melon Berry, Silkworm Thorn, zhe
- Durian (*Duria*; Malvaceae)
- Goumi (*Elaeagnus multiflora ovata*; Elaeagnaceae family)
- Hardy Kiwi (*Actinidia arguta*; Actinidiaceae family)
- Kiwifruit or Chinese gooseberry (*Actinidia* spp.; Actinidiaceae)
- Mock Strawberry or Indian Strawberry (*Potentilla indica*; Rosaceae)
- Lanzones
- Lapsi (*Choerospondias axillaris Roxb.* Anacardiaceae)
- Longan

- Lychee
- Mangosteen (*Garcinia mangostana*; Clusiaceae family)
- Nungu (*Borassus flabellifer*; Arecaceae)
- Peach
- Persimmon (aka Sharon Fruit) (*Diospyros kaki*; Ebenaceae)
- Rhubarb (*Rheum rhaponticum*; Polygonaceae)
- Sageretia (*Sageretia theezans*; Rhamnaceae) Also called Mock Buckthorn

FRUITS OF NORTH AMERICAN ORIGIN

(Includes Canada and the United States and all other countries that produce these fruits) Some other fruits native to North America that are eaten in a small way:

- American grape: North American species (e.g., *Vitis labrusca*; Vitaceae) and American-European hybrids are grown where grape (*Vitis vinifera*) is not hardy and are used as rootstocks
- American Mayapple (*Podophyllum peltatum*; Berberidaceae)
- American persimmon (*Diospyros virginiana*; Ebenaceae)
- Beach Plum (*Prunus maritima*; Rosaceae)
- Blueberry (*Vaccinium, sect. Cyanococcus*; Ericaceae)
- Buffaloberry (*Shepherdia argenta*; Elaeagnaceae), which grows wild in the prairies of Canada
- Chokecherry (*Prunus virginiana*; Rosaceae)
- Cocoplum (*Chrysobalanus icaco*; Chrysobalanaceae)
- Cranberry (*Vaccinium oxycoccus*; Ericaceae)
- False-mastic (*Mastichodendron foetidissimum*; Sapotaceae)
- Ground Plum (*Astragalus caryocarpus*; Fabaceae), also called Ground-plum milk-vetch
- Pawpaw (*Asimina triloba*; Annonaceae, not to be confused with Papaya (*Carica papaya*; Caricaceae), which is called pawpaw in some English dialects)

- Persimmon (*Diospyros virginiana*; Ebenaceae), also called native persimmon, American persimmon, or common persimmon
- Pigeon plum (*Coccoloba diversifolia*; Polygonaceae)
- Salal berry (*Gaultheria shallon*; Ericaceae)
- Salmonberry (*Rubus spectabilis*; Rosaceae)
- Saw Palmetto (*Serenoa repens*; Arecaceae)
- Texas persimmon (*Diospyros texana*; Ebenaceae)
- Thimbleberry (*Rubus parviflorus*; Rosaceae)
- Toyon (*Heteromeles arbutifolia*; Rosaceae)

FRUITS OF AUSTRALIAN ORIGIN

Although the fruits of Australia were eaten for thousands of years as bushfood by Aboriginal people, they have only been recently recognized for their culinary qualities by non-indigenous people. Many are regarded for their piquancy and spice-like qualities for use in cooking and preserves. Some Australian fruits also have exceptional nutritional qualities, including high vitamin C and other antioxidants.

- Atherton Raspberry (*Rubus probus*; Rosaceae)
- Black Apple (*Planchonella australis*; Sapotaceae)
- Blue tongue (*Melastoma affine*; Melastomataceae)
- Bolwarra (*Eupomatia laurina*; Eupomatiaceae)
- Burdekin Plum (*Pleiogynium timorense*; Anacardiaceae)
- Broad-leaf Bramble (*Rubus hillii*; Rosaceae)
- Cedar Bay cherry (*Eugenia carissoides*; Myrtaceae)
- Cluster fig (*Ficus racemosa*; Moraceae)
- Common apple-berry (*Billardiera scandens*; Pittosporaceae)
- Conkerberry (*Carissa lanceolata*; Apocynaceae)
- Davidson's plum (*Davidsonia* spp.; Cunoniaceae)
- Desert fig (*Ficus platypoda*; Moraceae)

- Desert lime (*Citrus glauca*; Rutaceae)
- Doubah (*Marsdenia australis*; Apocynaceae)
- Emu Apple (*Owenia acidula*; Meliaceae)
- Fibrous Satinash (*Syzygium fibrosum*; Myrtaceae)
- Finger Lime (*Citrus australasica*; Rutaceae)
- Illawarra Plum (*Podocarpus elatus*; Podocarpaceae)
- Little gooseberry tree (*Buachanania arborescens*; Anacardiaceae)
- Kakadu lime (*Citrus gracilis*; Rutaceae)
- Kutjera (*Solanum centrale*; Solanaceae)
- Kakadu plum (*Terminalia ferdinandiana*; Combretaceae)
- Karkalla (*Carpobrotus rossii*; Aizoaceae)
- Lady apple (*Syzygium suborbiculare*; Myrtaceae)
- Lemon aspen (*Acronychia acidula*; Rutaceae)
- Midyim (*Austromyrtus dulcis*; Myrtaceae)
- Mountain pepper (*Tasmannia* spp.; Winteraceae)
- Muntries (*Kunzea pomifera*; Myrtaceae)
- Native Cherry (*Exocarpus cupressiformis*; Santalaceae)
- Native currant (*Acrotriche depressa*; Ericaceae)
- Native gooseberry (*Physalis minima*; Solanaceae)
- Pigface (*Carpobrotus glaucescens*; Aizoaceae)
- Pink-flowered Native Raspberry (*Rubus parvifolius*; Rosaceae)
- Purple apple-berry (*Billarderia longiflora*; Pittosporaceae)
- Quandong (*Santalum acuminatum*; Elaeocarpaceae)
- Riberry (*Syzygium luehmannii*; Myrtaceae)
- Rose-leaf Bramble (*Rubus rosifolius*; Rosaceae)
- Rose myrtle (*Archirhodomyrtus beckleri*; Myrtaceae)

- Sandpaper Fig (*Ficus coronata*; Moraceae)
- Small-leaf tamarind (*Diploglottis campbellii*; Sapindaceae)
- Snow berry (*Gaultheria hispida*; Ericaceae)
- Sweet apple-berry (*Billarderia cymosa*; Pittosporaceae)
- Tanjong (*Mimusops elengi*; Sapindaceae)
- White aspen (*Acronychia oblongifolia*; Rutaceae)
- Wild orange (*Capparis mitchellii*; Capparaceae)
- Wongi (*Manilkara kaukii*; Sapotaceae)
- Yellow plum (*Ximenia americana*; Olacaceae)
- Zig Zag Vine (*Melodurum leichhardtii*; Annonaceae)

CACTI AND OTHER SUCCULENTS

Several cacti yield edible fruits, which are important traditional foods for some Native American peoples:

- Cardón (*Pachycereus pringlei*; Cactaceae)
- Dragonfruit (*Hylocereus undatus*; Cactaceae), also called pitaya
- Prickly pear (*Opuntia* spp.; Cactaceae)
- Saguaro (*Carnegiea gigantea*; Cactaceae)
- numerous other species of cacti

PODOCARPS

Podocarps are conifers in the family Podocarpaceae. The seed cones are highly modified and, in some, the seed is surrounded by fleshy scale tissue, resembling a drupe. These berry-like cone scales are eaten by birds which then disperse the seeds in their droppings and the cones can be eaten in many species. Podocarps are either half-hardy or frost tender, depending on species. Many genera are similar in that they have edible "fruits" and often don't have a common name.

- Kahikatea (*Dacrycarpus dacrydioides*)
- Manoao (*Manoao colensoi*)

- Nageia (*Nageia* spp.)
- Podocarpus (*Podocarpus* spp.)
- Prumnopitys (*Prumnopitys* spp.)
- Rimu (*Dacrydium cupressinum*)

HERBACEOUS ANNUALS FRUITS

Melons and Other Members of Cucurbitaceae or Solanaceae Family

Some exceptions to the statement that temperate fruits grow on woody perennials are:

- Gourds, (usually regarded as vegetables in cuisine) including, but not limited to:
- Butternut squash (*Cucurbita moschata*)
- Cushaw squash (*Cucurbita mixta*)
- Hubbard squash, Buttercup squash (*Cucurbita maxima*)
- Pumpkin, Acorn squash, Zucchini, Summer squash (*Cucurbita pepo*varieties)
- Horned melon (*Cucumis metuliferus*)
- Melon (*Cucumis melo*): cantaloupe, galia, and other muskmelons, honeydew

Accessory Fruits

The accessory fruits, seed organs which are not botanically berries at all:

- Raisin tree (*Hovenia dulcis*, Rhamnaceae) Also called Japanese Raisin Tree
- Strawberry (*Fragaria* spp.; Rosaceae)

MEDITERRANEAN AND SUBTROPICAL FRUITS

Fruits in this category are not hardy to extreme cold, as the preceding temperate fruits are, yet tolerate some frost and may have a modest chilling requirement. Notable among these are natives of the Mediterranean:

- Black mulberry (*Morus nigra*; Moraceae)
- Cornelian cherry (*Cornus mas*; Cornaceae)
- Date palm (*Phoenix dactylifera*; Arecaceae)
- Fig (*Ficus* spp. Moraceae)
- Grape, called raisin, sultana, or currant when it is dried. (*Vitis* spp.; Vitaceae)
- Jujube (*Ziziphus zizyphus*; Rhamnaceae)
- Olive (*Olea europea*; Oleaceae)
- Pomegranate (*Punica granatum*; Punicaceae)
- Sycamore fig (*Ficus* sycomorus. Moraceae) also called old world sycomore or just sycomore.

In the important genus *Citrus* (Rutaceae), some members are tropical, tolerating no frost. All common species of commerce are somewhat hardy:

- Blood Orange
- Citron (*Citrus medica*)
- Clementine (*Citrus reticulata* var. Clementine)
- Grapefruit (*Citrus paradisi*)
- Hybrids of the preceding species, such as the Orangelo, Tangelo, Rangpur (fruit) and Ugli fruit
- Kumquat (*Fortunella*)
- Lemon (*Citrus limon*)
- Limes
- Kaffir lime (*Citrus hystix*)
- Key Lime (*Citrus aurantifolia*)
- Persian lime Also known as tahiti lime.
- Mandarin (*Citrus reticulata*)
- Orange, of which there are sweet (*Citrus sinensis*) and sour (*Citrus aurantium*) species

- Pomelo (also known as the shaddock) (*Citrus maxima*)
- Sweet Lemon (*Citrus limetta*)
- Tangerine, and similar

Other Subtropical Fruits

- Avocado (*Persea americana*; Lauraceae)
- Carob (*Ceratonia siliqua*; Fabaceae)
- Feijoa (*Feijoa sellowiana*; Myrtaceae)
- Guava (*Psidium guajava*; Myrtaceae)
- Kumquat (*Fortunella* spp.; Rutaceae)
- Longan (*Euphoria longan*; Sapindaceae)
- Lúcuma (*Pouteria lucuma*; Sapotaceae)
- Lychee (*Litchi chinensis*; Sapindaceae)
- Passion fruit or Grenadilla (*Passiflora edulis* and other *Passiflora* spp.; Passifloraceae) Galendar in some part of east India (Darjeeling)
- Peanut (*Arachis hypogaea*; Fabaceae)
- Pond-apple (*Annona glabra*; Annonaceae) Also called Alligator-apple and Monkey-apple
- Strawberry guava (*Psidium litorale*; Myrtaceae)
- Tamarillo or Tree Tomato (*Cyphomandra betacea*; Solanaceae)
- Ugni (*Ugni molinae*; Myrtaceae)
- Yangmei (*Myrica rubra*; Myricaceae) Also called Yumberry, Yamamomo, Chinese Bayberry, Japanese Bayberry, Red Bayberry, or Chinese strawberry tree

TROPICAL FRUITS

Tropical fruit grow on plants of all habitats. The only characteristic that they share is an intolerance of frost.

- Acerola (*Malpighia glabra*; Malpighiaceae), also called West Indian Cherry or Barbados Cherry

- Ackee (*Blighia sapida* or *Cupania sapida*; Sapindaceae)
- African cherry orange (*Citropsis schweinfurthii*; Rutaceae)
- Amazon Grape (*Pourouma cecropiaefolia*; Moraceae)
- Araza
- Avocado
- Açaí (*Euterpe oleracea*; Arecaceae), or assai
- Babaco (*Carica pentagona*; Caricaceae)
- Bael (*Aegle marmelos*; Rutaceae)
- Banana (*Musacea* spp.; Musaceae); its starchy variant is the plantain
- Barbadine (granadilla; maracujá-açu in Portuguese)
- Barbados Cherry (*Malpighia glabra L.*; Malpighiaceae), also called Acerola, West Indian Cherry
- Betel Nut
- Bilimbi (*Averrhoa bilimbi*; Oxalidaceae) Also called cucumber tree or tree sorrel
- Bitter gourd
- Black sapote
- Bottle gourd also known as Calabash (*Lagenaria siceraria*; Cucurbitaceae)
- Brazil nut
- Breadfruit (*Artocarpus altilis*; Moraceae)
- Burmese grape, or Latka (*Baccaurea sapida*; Phyllanthaceae)
- Calabashtree
- CamuCamu (*Myrciaria dubia*; Myrtaceae)
- Canistel
- Cape gooseberry
- Carambola (*Averrhoa carambola*; Oxalidaceae), also called star fruit or *five fingers*

- Cashew
- Cempedak or Champedak (*Artocarpus champeden*; Moraceae)
- Ceylon gooseberry
- Chenet (guinep or ackee; pitomba-das-Guinas in Portuguese), also known as Spanish Lime or mamoncillo
- Cherimoya (*Annona cherimola*; Annonaceae)
- Chili pepper
- Caimito (caimite; related to the yellow abiu - egg fruit)
- Cacao
- Coffee
- Cupuaçu
- Custard apple (*Annona reticulata*; Annonaceae), also called *Bullock's Heart*
- Damson plum (*Chrysophyllum oliviforme*; Sapotaceae), also called *Satin Leaf*
- Date
- Date-plum (*Diospyros lotus*; Ebenaceae)
- Dragonfruit (*Hylocereus* spp.; Cactaceae), also called pitaya
- Durian (*Durio spp.*; Bombacaceae)
- Eggfruit (*Pouteria campechiana*; Sapotaceae), also called canistel or yellow sapote
- Elephant apple (*Dillenia indica*; Dilleniaceae)
- Giant granadilla
- Golden Apple
- Guarana (*Paullinia cupana*; Sapindaceae)
- Guava
- Guavaberry or Rumberry; (*Myrciaria floribunda*; Myrtaceae)
- Hog plum (taperebá in Portuguese)

- Horned melon (*Cucumis metuliferus*; Cucurbitaceae)
- Huito (*Genipa americana*; Rubiaceae); also called *jagua*, *genipap*, jenipapo
- Indian almond
- Indian fig
- Indian jujube
- Indian Prune (*Flacourtia rukan*; Flacourtiaceae)
- Jaboticaba (*Myrciaria cauliflora*; Myrtaceae), also called Brazilian Grape Tree
- Jackfruit (*Artocarpus heterophyllus* Moraceae), also called *nangka*
- Jambul (*Syzygium cumini*; Myrtaceae)
- Jatobá (*Hymenae coubaril*; Leguminosae) Caesalpinioideae)
- Jocote, also called Jamaica Plum
- Kandis (*Garcinia forbesii*; Clusiaceae)
- Keppel fruit (*Stelechocarpus burakol*; Annonaceae)
- Kumquat
- Kundong (*Garcinia sp.*; Clusiaceae)
- Lablab
- Langsat (*Lansium domesticum*), also called longkong or duku
- Lansones (*Lansium domesticum* spp.; Meliaceae)
- Lemon
- Leucaena
- Lime
- Longan
- Loquat
- Lucuma
- Lychee

- Mabolo (*Diospyros discolor*; Ebenaceae) also known as a velvet persimmon
- Macadamia, also known as a Queensland nut
- Mamey sapote (*Pouteria sapota*; Sapotaceae); also known as *mamee apple*; abricó in Portuguese
- Mamoncillo (*Melicoccus bijugatus*; Sapindaceae), also known as quenepa, genip or Fijian Longan
- Mandarin
- Manila tamarind (or Monkeypod, *Pithecellobium dulce*)
- Mango (*Mangifera indica*; Anacardiaceae)
- Mangosteen (*Garcinia mangostana*; Clusiaceae)
- Marang (*Artocarpus odoratissima*; Moraceae), a breadfruit relative
- Melinjo
- Melon pear
- Monstera (*Monstera deliciosa*; Araceae) also called Swiss Cheese Plant, Split-leaf Philodendron
- Morinda
- Mountain soursop
- Mundu
- Mung bean
- Muskmelon
- Nance
- Naranjilla, Lulo (*Solanum quitoense*; Solanaceae)
- Nutmeg
- Neem
- Oil Palm
- Okra
- Papaya (*Carica papaya*; Caricaceae)

- Peach palm
- Peanut butter fruit (*Bunchosia argentea*; Malpighiaceae)
- Pequi or Souari Nut (*Caryocar brasiliense*; Caryocaraceae)
- Pewa (peach palm; pupunha in Portuguese)
- Pigeon pea
- Pili nut
- Pineapple (*Ananas comosus* or *Ananas sativas*; Bromeliaceae)
- Pitomba (*Eugenia luschnathiana* or *Talisia esculenta*)
- Plantain
- Poha or Cape Gooseberry (*Physalis peruviana*; Solanaceae)
- Pois doux (*Inga edulis*, *ice-cream bean*, or *inga-cipó* in Portuguese)
- Poisonleaf (*Dichapetalum cymosum*) (?)
- Pommecythère or pomcité (*Spondias cytherea*); also known as golden apple, June plum or Jew plum and ambarella, and as cajamanga in Portuguese
- Pommerac (*Eugenia malaccensis*); also known as Otaheite apple; Malay apple; jambo in Portuguese
- Pulasan
- Pummelo
- Pupunha or peach-palm (*Bactris gasipaes*; Palmae); also known as *pewa*
- Rambutan (*Nephelium lappaceum*; Sapindaceae)
- Red Mombin (*Spondias purpurea*; Anacardiaceae)
- Riberry (*Syzygium luehmannii*; Myrtaceae), also called Lilly Pilly, Lillipilli, Chinese Apple
- Ridged gourd
- Salak (*Salacca edulis*), also called snakefruit
- Santol (*Sandoricum koetjape*; Meliaceae)
- Sapodilla (*Achras/Manilkara zapota*; Sapotaceae), also called chiku, mespel, naseberry, sapadilla, snake fruit, sawo

- Sea grape
- Soncoya (*Annona diversifolia*)
- Soursop (*Annona muricata*; Annonaceae), also called guanabana
- Soybean
- Star apple (*Chrysophyllum cainito*), also called caimito or *caimite*
- Strawberry guava
- Strawberry pear
- Sugar apple (*Annona squamosa*; Annonaceae); ata in Portuguese
- Summer squash
- Surinam Cherry (*Eugenia uniflora*; Myrtaceae) also called Brazilian Cherry, Cayenne Cherry, Pitanga
- Sweet granadilla
- Sweet orange
- Sweet pepper
- Sweetsop
- Rose apple (*Syzygium jambos*; Myrtaceae), also called Malay apple
- Tamarind (*Tamarindus indica*; Caesalpiniaceae)
- Vanilla
- Water apple
- Watermelon
- Wax apple (*Syzygium samarangense*)
- Wax gourd
- White sapote
- Winged bean

Index

L

M